THE USBORNE BIG BOOK OF EXPERIMENTS

THE USBORNE BIG BOOK OF EXPERIMENTS

EDITED BY ALASTAIR SMITH

DESIGNED BY FIONA JOHNSON

PHOTOGRAPHY BY HOWARD ALLMAN

COVER DESIGNED BY AMANDA BARLOW

SCHOLASTIC INC.

New York   Toronto   London   Auckland   Sydney
Mexico City   New Delhi   Hong Kong   Buenos Aires

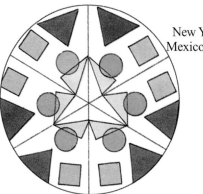

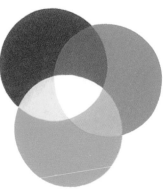

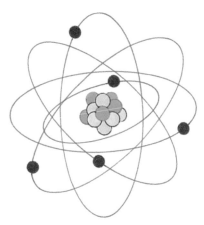

Contents

THE WORLD AROUND YOU

In this section you can perform experiments on many everyday things – and create some surprising results.

For instance you can find out how to test for acids by using a cabbage. Also, you can see how to make bubbling gases by adding a little baking soda to some vinegar.

⚠️

To avoid the possibility of harming yourself, be careful whenever you see a red warning triangle next to an instruction.

Testing the water

All things are made up of tiny particles, called molecules. These tend to pull each other together, stopping things from breaking up. You can see how molecules pull together by looking closely at the surface of a glass of water as you do these experiments.

Needle on water

You will need
- Drinking glass • Needle • Tissue paper
- Water

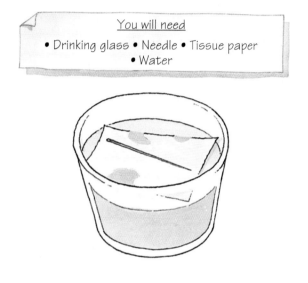

Fill the glass with water. Put the needle on the small piece of tissue paper and lay it gently on the water. Eventually the tissue will sink, but what happens to the needle?

What happens?

The tissue paper sinks, but the needle is so light that it is supported by the water's surface. The molecules of water at the surface hold together with such strength that they form a kind of skin (called surface tension) which the needle cannot break. Look closely and you will see that the needle actually dents the water's skin.

Bulging water

You will need
- Drinking glass • Water • Small coins

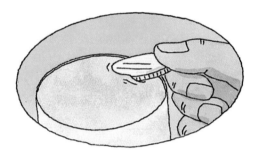

Fill the glass to the brim with water. Gently slide in some coins, one at a time. What happens to the surface of the water as you add the coins?

What happens?

It is best to use small coins for this experiment, so that you can raise the surface gradually.

If you add the coins gradually, the water should bulge above the glass without tumbling down the side. The molecules pull together with enough force to stop the water from spilling. If you keep adding coins, though, the water above the glass will become so great that the molecules will break apart and the water will spill.

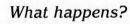
What is a molecule made of?

All molecules are made of even tinier particles, called atoms. There are just over one hundred different types of atoms. They make up everything that exists in the entire universe.

This diagram shows the structure of a molecule of water. It is made of three atoms: two hydrogen and one oxygen.

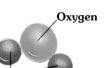

Oxygen

Hydrogen

All water molecules have this structure.

Changing surface tension

<u>You will need</u>
- Small spoon • Water • Clean table top
- Drinking straw • Dishwashing liquid

It's a fact!
Some very small, light animals, such as pond skaters, can walk on water's skin.

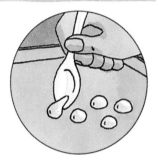

1. Dip the spoon in some water and then drip it onto the table top. The water should hold together in little dome shapes.

2. Touch the droplets with the straw dipped in dishwashing liquid. What happens to the water as soon as you touch it with the soapy straw?

What happens?

The chemicals in the dishwashing liquid cause the water molecules to hold together less strongly. So the molecules move apart more easily and the water spreads out.

Blowing bubbles

<u>You will need</u>
- Large spoon • Water • Dishwashing liquid
- Thin wire, such as florists' wire

It's a fact!
Over three-quarters of the Earth is covered by water.

1. First make a mixture of water and dishwashing liquid. For every large spoonful of water that you use, mix in three large spoonfuls of dishwashing liquid.

2. Make a loop out of the thin wire and dip it into the mixture. You will see a thin film of soapy water stretch across the loop. Blow gently onto the liquid. What do you see happening?

What happens?

The soapy water stretches out into a very thin skin across the wire loop. When you blow on it, the watery skin stretches out as far as it possibly can until it forms a bubble shape.

Changing states

Everything in the world is either a solid, liquid or gas. Some substances, such as water, can be changed easily from solid to liquid (or from liquid to gas) and back again. The experiments on these two pages investigate how this happens.

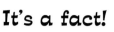
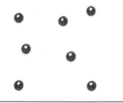
Make water disappear and reappear

This simple experiment shows how you can make water turn into gas and then back into water again. To make it work you'll need to choose a sunny day for your investigation.

> ### You will need
> • 2 big plates • Book • Water • Cup
> • Metal container with shiny surface • Ice cubes

1. Put one big plate on a sunny windowsill. Pour cold water onto the plate and leave it for three to four hours. Look at it every 30 minutes and you will see that the water gradually disappears.

2. Now put two plates on the windowsill. Pour about half a cup of water onto each one. Shade one plate with the book. Look at the plates after about an hour. Which has the most water?

3. Fill up the metal container with lots of ice cubes. Stand it in a warm place and leave it for a few minutes. Then take a look at the container. What is on the outside of the container?

What happens?

When water is warmed, it evaporates (water molecules rise to become part of the gases in the air). The plate in the shade stays cooler than the other one so the water on it evaporates at a slower rate.

Warm air usually contains lots of water molecules. When the warm air touches something cold these molecules collect back into big drops that you can see. This is called condensation.

INSTANT EXPERT

What makes solids, liquids and gases different from each other?

Everything is made up of tiny particles called molecules. Molecules are always moving, even in things that look still. Whether something is a solid, a liquid or a gas depends on how much its molecules are moving around.

Molecules in solids are packed together very tightly in fixed positions. This makes it difficult for the solid to change shape.

In liquids, molecules are close together but they can slide past one another and change places. Because of this, liquids can change shape easily.

Molecules in gases are very widely spaced, so gases can fit into different shapes very easily. They can also be squashed easily.

Making a hole in ice

Put a pinch of salt on the top of the ice cube. Leave it in a cold place for ten minutes. Does the ice change in any way?

Salt

Salty ice melts first.

Pure ice stays frozen longer.

What happens?

Ice made from pure water does not melt until it reaches 0°C (32°F). This is called its melting point. When you add salt to ice, it lowers the melting point so the ice starts to melt when it is colder than 0°C (32°F). The salty part of the ice cube changes into water, while the rest stays frozen.

Strong ice

Usually, when a liquid turns to a solid, it shrinks and takes up less space. Do this experiment to see if water behaves in the same way.

You will need
• Small, clean metal container with a resealable lid • Bottle top
• 3 pencils • Adhesive tape
• Water • Freezer

What happens?

When water cools and turns into ice it gets bigger. As it gets bigger it presses against the container. It pushes so hard that it forces the lid up and breaks the pencil. The expanding ice is so strong that the container's sides may get pushed out as well.

Press on the lid after adding the water.

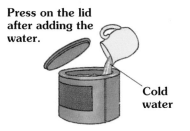

Cold water

1. First, take the metal container. Fill it up to the top with cold water, so that there is hardly any room for air in the container. Press the lid on as hard as you can.

Adhesive tape

Pencils

Bottle top

Tape

2. Put the bottle top on the lid. Put two pencils under the container and one on the bottle top. Wind tape around the pencils. Freeze for about eight hours. Does anything happen?

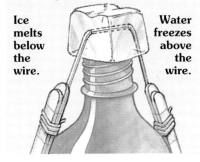

Sinking through ice

You will need
• Thin wire 20cm (8in) long
• Adhesive tape • Bottle
• Ice cube • 2 spoons

1. Wind the ends of the wire around the handles of two spoons and tape securely.

2. Balance an ice cube on the top of the bottle. Rest the wire across the ice cube so the spoons hang down equally on either side. Put the bottle in a cold place and watch what happens.

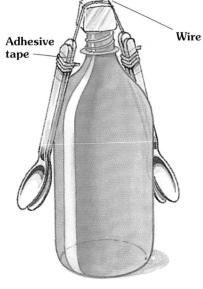

Adhesive tape

Wire

What happens?

When something presses on ice it lowers the melting point of the ice. The ice cube changes into water where the wire presses on it. As the wire sinks through the ice, the water above it should freeze again.

Ice melts below the wire.

Water freezes above the wire.

Bubbling up

There are hundreds of different gases. You cannot see or smell most of them, so you cannot tell that they are around you. On these pages you can find out how to make a gas that is in the air around you, called carbon dioxide.

Make carbon dioxide gas

You will need
• Cork • Skewer
• 2 flexible drinking straws
• Scissors • Drinking glass
• Food dye • Baking soda
• Vinegar • Bottle
• Small piece of paper

1. Make a hole through the middle of the cork using a skewer. Then push the flexible drinking straw down into the hole.

2. Cut a small slit in the other end of the straw and slide it inside the second straw, so that the two straws fit together tightly.

3. Fill the glass with water. Then stir in just a few drops of food dye, so that the water becomes tinted, but not too dark.

4. Pour half a tablespoon of baking soda down a folded piece of paper into the bottle (as shown at the top of page 11). Then pour in some vinegar until the bottle is about a quarter full.

5. Quickly push the cork into the top of the bottle and put the end of the second straw in the glass of dyed water. What happens in the water?

The gas can only escape through the straw held in the cork.

Gas is pushed along the straws as it is produced in the bottle.

What happens?

Baking soda contains a substance called a carbonate. When you mix a carbonate with an acid, such as vinegar, they make carbon dioxide gas. The gas builds up and is pushed along the straw into the water. It comes to the surface in bubbles.

Bubbles of carbon dioxide gas come out into the glass.

The vinegar and baking soda bubble furiously in the bottle.

Make a fire extinguisher

Flames need a gas called oxygen to burn. This experiment shows you what happens to a flame when it is surrounded by carbon dioxide.

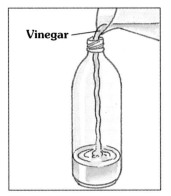

Vinegar

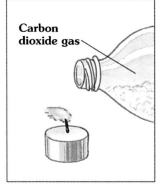

Baking soda

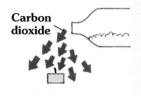

Carbon dioxide gas

1. Put the candle on the plate and light it. Then pour five tablespoons of vinegar into the small glass bottle.

2. Using a folded piece of paper as a funnel, pour half a tablespoon of baking soda down into the bottle. The mixture should fizz.

3. Now hold the bottle sideways over the candle, making sure no liquid pours out. What happens to the flame?

What happens?

The acid and baking soda react to make carbon dioxide gas. Carbon dioxide is heavier than air so it pushes the air away from the candle. Without oxygen from the air the flame will go out.

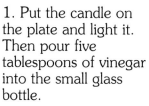

Carbon dioxide

More ways to make carbon dioxide

There are lots of things you can mix to make carbon dioxide. For example, you could take anything from list A (which contains acids only) and mix it with anything from list B (which contains carbonates only). You will always make carbon dioxide.

List A
• Vinegar
• Lemon juice
• Grapefruit juice
• Cola drink
(left open to settle for 10 minutes)
• Sour milk

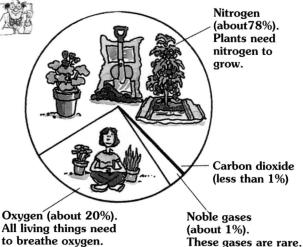

List B
• Baking soda
• Limestone
• Crushed eggshell
• Washing soda*

INSTANT EXPERT

Is air a gas?

The air you breathe is a mixture of several gases. The main ones are nitrogen, oxygen and carbon dioxide. This picture shows you the amounts of different gases that there are in the air around you.

Nitrogen (about 78%). Plants need nitrogen to grow.

Carbon dioxide (less than 1%)

Oxygen (about 20%). All living things need to breathe oxygen.

Noble gases (about 1%). These gases are rare.

It's a fact!

Plants help to keep the balance of oxygen and carbon dioxide gases in the air. In daylight they take in carbon dioxide and send out oxygen. At night they take in oxygen and send out carbon dioxide.

* Washing soda can burn you, so be very careful not to get it on your skin if you use it.

Expanding and contracting

When things get warmer they usually get bigger, or expand. When they get cooler they get smaller, or contract. The tests on these pages show that this happens.

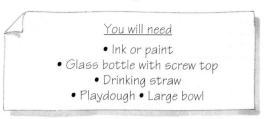

<u>You will need</u>
- Ink or paint
- Glass bottle with screw top
- Drinking straw
- Playdough • Large bowl

Bottle fountain

1. Remove the screw top from the glass bottle and make a hole in it with a pair of scissors.

2. Half fill the bottle with water containing a few drops of ink. Screw the top on as tightly as possible.

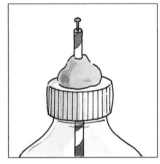

3. Push the straw through the hole. Press playdough around it to seal up the hole. Put a plug of playdough in the end of the straw.

4. Put the bottle in a large bowl and fill it up with hot water. Leave it for a few minutes. What happens to the bottled water?

What happens?

The hot water in the bowl warms the air in the bottle. As the air is warmed it expands and pushes the water up the straw and out in a spray.

This experiment is messy, so it's best to do it outside. Alternatively, you might like to do it while you are taking a bath.

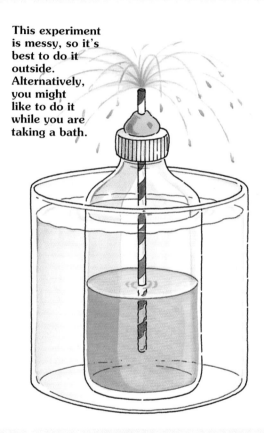

Cooling and shrinking

<u>You will need</u>
- Plastic bottle with screw top
- Ice cubes
- Plastic bag

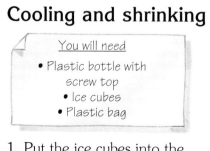

1. Put the ice cubes into the plastic bag and crush them. Put the ice in the plastic bottle. Screw on the lid.

2. Shake the bottle, then put it down. What happens to the bottle as the ice cools the air inside it?

What happens?

As the air cools, it contracts. Because of this it takes up less and less space. As a result, when the air shrinks the bottle's sides are pulled in.

Magic balloon bottle

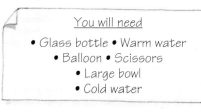

1. Fill the glass bottle with warm water. Leave it for a few minutes to warm the bottle. Pour out the water.

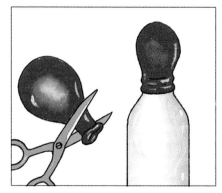

2. Cut the neck off the balloon. Stretch it over the top of the bottle. Then stand the bottle in a bowl of cold water. What happens to the balloon?

What happens?

As the air in the bottle gets cooler it contracts. As it contracts, it takes up less room in the bottle. To make up the extra room in the bottle, air from outside pushes into the bottle. Because the balloon is in the way, it gets pushed into the bottle too.

For the most impressive results use a big bottle. Try to cool the bottle as much as you can.

INSTANT EXPERT

Why do things expand and contract?

The tiny particles (called molecules) that make up all things are always moving. If they are heated up they move faster. This makes them try and pull away from each other, so the thing they make up gets bigger (expands). As molecules cool, they slow down. When they slow down they use less room, so the thing that they make up gets smaller (contracts).

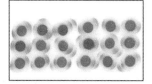

Heated molecules. As they get warmer, they move faster and farther apart.

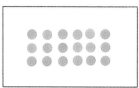

Cooled molecules. As they become cooler, they slow down and don't use so much room.

Growing crystals

Some substances, such as salt, sugar and washing soda are made up of tiny pieces, all the same shape, called crystals. On these two pages you can find out how to make crystals grow. They will take a few days, but the results are worth waiting for.

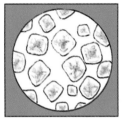

Viewed under a microscope, crystals of table salt look like this.

Grow your own crystals

You will need
- Clean glass jar • Piece of thread • Teaspoon
- Washing soda* • Paper clip • Bowl
- Metal spoon • Hot water • Pencil

1. Put the metal spoon into a jar. Then, almost fill the jar with some hot water. The spoon should protect the jar by preventing the hot water from cracking the glass.

2. Put several teaspoons of washing soda into the water and stir until it has all disappeared. Put in several more teaspoons of soda and stir again vigorously.

3. Stand the jar in a bowl of hot water to keep the water in the jar hot. Spoon in more soda and stir again. Stir in soda until no more will disappear in the water.

4. Tie the paper clip onto one end of the thread. Tie the other end to the pencil. Drop the clip into the jar and wind the thread around the pencil until the clip hangs as shown.

Try mixing a few drops of poster paint or ink in the water to make crystals in an eye-catching shade.

What happens?

As the water cools, it cannot hold the washing soda. So the soda starts to form crystals around the string. The rest of the soda is attracted to the crystals on the string, until a whole cluster forms. At the same time, the water evaporates into the air. As it does it leaves the soda behind, which forms into more and more crystals around the string.

14

* **Washing soda can burn you, so be very careful not to get it on your skin.**

Grow a crystal column

Here is a way to make pillars of washing soda grow up and down until they meet in the middle.

Washing soda

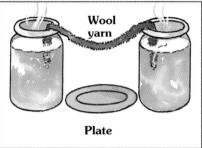

Wool yarn

Plate

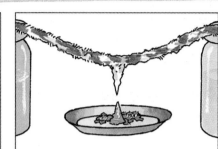

1. Fill two glass jars with warm water. Stir in lots of washing soda. Go on adding soda and stirring it until no more will disappear.

2. Put the jars in a warm place. Put the plate in between them. Drop the ends of the yarn rope into the jars so the middle hangs over the plate.

3. After a few days crystals will have grown along the rope and met in the middle. What happens after they have met on the rope?

As the water evaporates, the crystals also form in a pile on the plate.

What happens?

Water and soda from the jars is soaked up by the rope. It travels along and drips off the middle. As it drips, the water evaporates. The soda crystals are left behind clinging to the rope.

It's a fact!

Snowflakes are made of tiny ice crystals. The crystals come together differently each time, so no two snowflakes are the same.

INSTANT EXPERT

Why are crystals different shapes?

The particles that make up a crystal can be arranged and held together in a number of different ways. Because of this, crystals can come in a range of shapes and sizes. Six of the most common crystal shapes are shown on the right. If you look at sugar, salt or sand under a magnifying glass you will see the shapes of their crystals.

 Cubic

Rhombic

Tetragonal

 Monoclinic

Hexagonal

 Triclinic

Investigating acids and alkalis

Acids and alkalis are two important groups of chemicals. They are dangerous when they are strong but weaker kinds are found in lots of everyday things including food and drinks. Using a liquid called an indicator you can test things to find out whether they are acids or alkalis.

Acid attack

Strong acids and alkalis eat away at things and make them dissolve. Many buildings are eaten away by acid. Fumes from factories, power stations and traffic all contain acids that go into the air and fall as acid rain. Try this test to see how acid affects building materials.

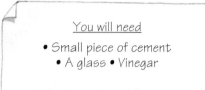

You will need
- Small piece of cement
- A glass • Vinegar

1. Take a small lump of dried cement and put it into a glass. Then pour in some vinegar to cover it.

Vinegar — **Cement**

2. Leave the experiment for two to three days. What do you think will happen to the cement?

What happens?

Vinegar is an acid. It eats away at the cement and makes it dissolve into the vinegar.

Make an acid indicator

To do the experiment on the next page you need to prepare some special indicator liquid, using the water from a boiled red cabbage. Keep the indicator fresh by storing it in a refrigerator.

You will need
- Half a red cabbage • Metal saucepan
- Wooden spoon • Large screw-top jar
- Strainer • Knife • Water

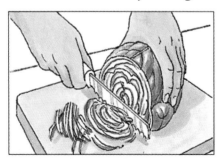

1. Carefully chop the cabbage into small pieces. Put the pieces in the saucepan with enough water to cover them.

2. Bring the water to boiling point. Turn off the heat, stir the cabbage mixture and leave it to cool for half an hour or so.

Cool indicator liquid

3. Pour the cabbage water through the strainer into the jar. The liquid in the jar is your indicator.

Red cabbage concoctions

This experiment can amaze your friends. First make some red cabbage indicator liquid by following the instructions on the previous page. After you've finished testing them don't drink them – they will taste horrible.

following the instructions on the previous page.

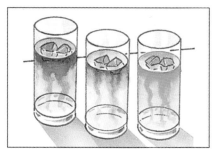

You will need
- Ice cube tray • 3 tall glasses
- Clear lemonade (or lemon juice mixed with water) • Water • Baking soda
- Teaspoon • Red cabbage indicator liquid

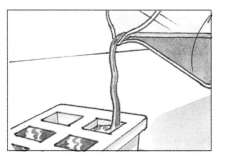

1. Pour red cabbage indicator liquid into the compartments of the ice cube tray. Freeze the liquid for about half an hour until it forms ice cubes.

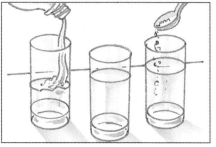

2. Fill the three tall glasses, one with water, one with lemonade and one with some tap water mixed with a teaspoon of baking soda.

3. Now drop two indicator ice cubes into each glass. How do the "drinks" change? Do they look the same when the ice has completely dissolved?

What happens?

Because it is an acid, lemonade turns the indicator reddish-pink.

Baking soda turns the indicator blue-green. This is because it is an alkali.

Water is neutral (neither an acid nor an alkali) so the indicator stays purple.

Lemonade   **Baking soda**   **Water**

INSTANT EXPERT

What happens when acids and alkalis mix?

When you mix an acid and an alkali, they make a different kind of chemical, called a salt. If you mix the right amount the acid and alkali cancel each other out and make a neutral salt (neither acidic nor alkaline). Neutral salts do not sting or eat away at things. Table salt is one kind of neutral salt.

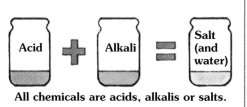

Acid + Alkali = Salt (and water)

All chemicals are acids, alkalis or salts.

Chemistry in the kitchen

Cooking involves chemistry. By mixing things together and cooking them you cause chemical changes that give you something totally different from what you started with.

Making yeast work

Yeast is made of millions of tiny living things called microbes. When they feed they make carbon dioxide gas. This experiment shows what happens when you mix yeast with flour and water and then cook it to make bread. (It will take about 20 minutes to prepare, two hours for the yeast to work and 20 minutes to bake.)

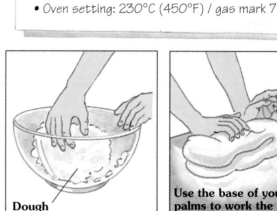

You will need
- Mug • Jug • Big mixing bowl • Teaspoon
- 2 baking trays • 2 large plastic bags
- Sugar • Salt • Flour • Butter
- Dried yeast • Warm water • Clean surface
- Oven setting: 230°C (450°F) / gas mark 7

Yeast mixture bubbles.

Mix with your fingers (but wash them first).

Dough

Use the base of your palms to work the dough.

1. Pour a mug of warm water into the jug. Stir in a teaspoon of sugar. Sprinkle in two teaspoons of dried yeast, then wait for ten minutes. The mixture should fill with bubbles.

2. Pour three mugs of flour into the big mixing bowl and stir in a teaspoon of salt. Make a hole in the middle, then pour in the frothy yeast mixture.

3. Use your fingers to blend the mixture into a squashy lump, called dough. Wipe the dough around the bowl to pick up all the flour. Then put it on a clean, floured surface.

4. Stretch, fold and punch the dough using your knuckles and palms. This is called kneading. After ten minutes your dough should feel smooth and springy.

Plastic bag

Tuck bag under bowl.

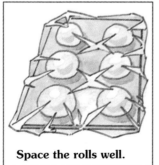

Space the rolls well.

Wear oven gloves. ⚠

5. Put the dough back in the bowl and cover it with a plastic bag. Put the bowl somewhere warm. After 90 minutes the dough should have risen to twice its original size.

6. Knead the dough for a few minutes, then shape it into 12 rolls. Put the rolls on baking trays smeared with butter. Cover the trays with plastic bags and wait 30 minutes.

7. Warm up the oven. Then bake the rolls until they are crisp and brown on top and sound hollow when tapped underneath. Finally, let them cool.

What happens?

Flour contains a substance called gluten. When you knead dough, you make the gluten into a soft, stretchy network.

Yeast feeds on sugar and flour, making carbon dioxide gas. This gets trapped in the gluten network so the dough rises.

The oven's heat kills the yeast and hardens the gluten network. The carbon dioxide bubbles escape, leaving the bread full of tiny holes.

Watching yeast

Dried yeast looks like lifeless granules, but this is because the millions of tiny microbes stay inactive as long as they are cool and dry.

You will need

• Dried yeast • Sugar
• Jug • Glass bottle
• Balloon • Bowl • Teaspoon
• Tablespoon • Warm water

1. Make a runny yeast mixture in the jug by mixing two teaspoons of yeast with two tablespoons of warm water. Then stir in a teaspoon of sugar.

2. Pour the yeast mixture into the bottle and stretch the balloon over its neck. Stand the bottle in a bowl of warm water for 15 minutes.

It's a fact!

In hot climates, you can cook an egg in the heat of the sun.

What happens?

As the yeast feeds, the carbon dioxide it produces fills the mixture with bubbles. These pop and the gas blows up the balloon.

Giant blue meringues

This experiment shows how you can turn eggs, sugar and a little food dye into something spectacular!

You will need

• 4 eggs • 220g (2 cups) sugar
• Large bowl • Blue food dye • Greased baking trays
• Oven setting: 110°C (225°F) / gas mark ¼

THIS IS QUITE TRICKY.

1. Set the oven to heat up. Separate the egg whites from the yolks (ask a grown-up to help you do this).

2. Whisk the egg whites in a large bowl. First they get fluffy, then they turn stiff and white.

3. When the egg white is stiff, add the sugar and stir it in gently. Then add a few drops of blue food dye.

4. Drop spoonfuls of the mixture in round, swirly shapes onto the greased baking trays. Put them in the oven for 2½ hours.

What happens?

When you whisk the egg whites, hundreds of tiny air bubbles get trapped in the mixture. Eventually there are so many bubbles that the mixture becomes a stiff foam.

The oven's heat makes the air bubbles expand and the foam puffs up. It also causes a chemical change in the egg white, making it solid. This is called coagulation.

Chemicals in your body

The food you eat is made of molecules that are too big to be used by your body. Your body makes special chemicals called enzymes to break them up. Here are two experiments to show how some of your body's enzymes work.

Egg eater experiment

This experiment uses detergent that contains enzymes similar to those in your stomach. It won't take long to prepare – but it will take a couple of days for the enzyme to work on the egg.

<table>
<tr><td align="center"><u>You will need</u>
• An egg • Detergent containing enzymes
• Detergent without enzymes • 2 glass jars • Pen
• Adhesive labels • Warm water • Knife • Large spoon</td></tr>
</table>

1. Boil some water and put an egg in it for 10 minutes or so until it becomes hard-boiled. Then let it cool completely before you peel it.

2. Put a large spoonful of detergent without enzymes in one jar and a large spoonful of detergent with enzymes in the other. Label both jars.

3. Put eight large spoonfuls of warm water into both of the jars and then stir vigorously until the detergent has disappeared.

4. Cut two pieces of egg white, exactly the same size, and put one in each jar. Put the jars somewhere warm and leave them for two days or so.

A good way to keep your jars warm would be to wrap them with cloths and put them next to some hot water pipes under the kitchen sink.

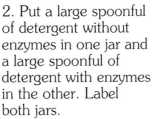

5. After two days, take the egg pieces out of the jars and examine them. The egg from the detergent with enzymes should be the smaller of the two.

What happens?

The enzymes in the detergent attack the molecules in the egg and break them into smaller molecules – which dissolve in water. (The piece of egg in the other jar shows that egg does not dissolve in ordinary detergent, and that it is the enzymes which eat the egg away.)

Egg   Enzyme

Spit test

Foods that come from plants, such as flour, contain a substance called starch. This test will show you what happens when starch mixes with your spit. The scientific name for spit is saliva.

You will need

• Flour • Iodine* • Mug • Teaspoon • Water
• Test tube (or small jar) • 2 jars • Eyedropper

1. First make an iodine solution. Pour a little iodine into a jar, then add the same amount of water to dilute it. You will need this to test for starch.

2. Put a teaspoon of flour in the mug and add a little cold water. Stir it thoroughly to make a smooth paste. Then fill the mug with boiling water.

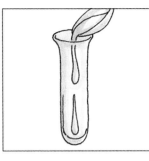

3. Let the flour solution cool down completely, then carefully dribble a teaspoon of it into the test tube. Do it over a sink so you avoid making a mess.

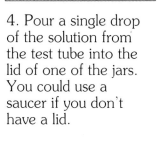

4. Pour a single drop of the solution from the test tube into the lid of one of the jars. You could use a saucer if you don't have a lid.

Stand the test tube in the other jar.

5. Drop iodine mixture onto the flour solution. The iodine should turn blue-black or brown. This shows that the solution contains some starch.

6. Now spit several times into the test tube. Cover the top of the tube and shake it vigorously to mix the flour solution and spit thoroughly.

Wash the lid after each test.

7. Put the test tube in a warm place. Every 20 minutes, pour out one drop of solution, test it with the iodine and see what shade the iodine turns.

8. After several hours you should find that the shade of the iodine hardly changes. This shows that there is very little starch left in the solution.

What happens?

The starch in the solution has been eaten away by your saliva. Saliva contains an enzyme called ptyalin (pronounced tie-a-lin) which attacks starch molecules and turns them into smaller molecules of another substance, which is called maltose.

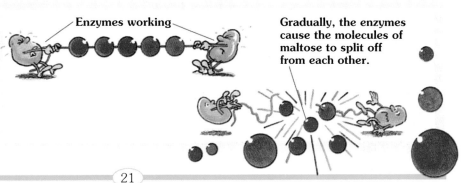

Enzymes working

Gradually, the enzymes cause the molecules of maltose to split off from each other.

* **You can buy iodine from a pharmacy.**

Splitting inks

Inks and dyes are made from chemicals. Below you can find out how to separate the chemicals in different inks to make amazing patterns.

Split the ink

1. Make an eye-catching drawing on some blotting paper. To ensure that your experiment gives the most dramatic effects, use as many different shades of felt-tip pens as you can.

2. Dip the bottom of the paper into a saucer of water. Make sure that the paper can't fall over and leave it for a few minutes. What happens to your drawing?

What happens?

As the water is soaked up by the blotting paper, it carries the inks with it. Different chemicals travel at different speeds so the chemicals in the inks separate, making patterns. Separating chemicals like this is called chromatography.

Dark shades like this contain more chemicals than lighter shades.

Different shades make different patterns.

Pictures using lots of different shades, such as this one, give the most dramatic effects.

Surprising black ink

How many chemicals do you think are used to make black ink? Try this test to find out.

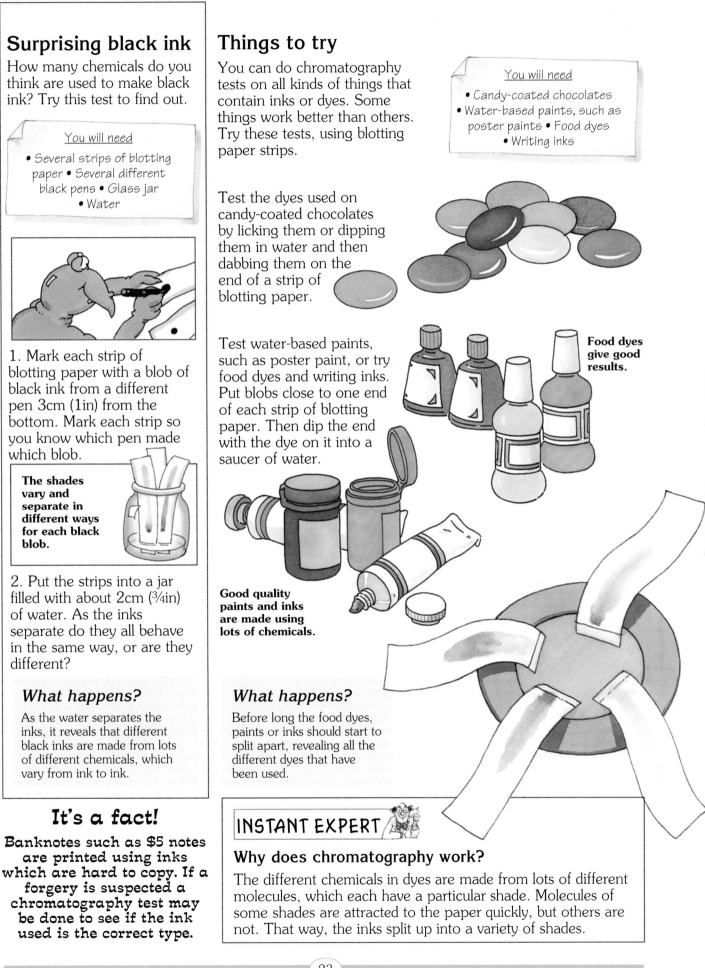

1. Mark each strip of blotting paper with a blob of black ink from a different pen 3cm (1in) from the bottom. Mark each strip so you know which pen made which blob.

The shades vary and separate in different ways for each black blob.

2. Put the strips into a jar filled with about 2cm (¾in) of water. As the inks separate do they all behave in the same way, or are they different?

What happens?

As the water separates the inks, it reveals that different black inks are made from lots of different chemicals, which vary from ink to ink.

It's a fact!

Banknotes such as $5 notes are printed using inks which are hard to copy. If a forgery is suspected a chromatography test may be done to see if the ink used is the correct type.

Things to try

You can do chromatography tests on all kinds of things that contain inks or dyes. Some things work better than others. Try these tests, using blotting paper strips.

Test the dyes used on candy-coated chocolates by licking them or dipping them in water and then dabbing them on the end of a strip of blotting paper.

Food dyes give good results.

Test water-based paints, such as poster paint, or try food dyes and writing inks. Put blobs close to one end of each strip of blotting paper. Then dip the end with the dye on it into a saucer of water.

Good quality paints and inks are made using lots of chemicals.

What happens?

Before long the food dyes, paints or inks should start to split apart, revealing all the different dyes that have been used.

INSTANT EXPERT

Why does chromatography work?

The different chemicals in dyes are made from lots of different molecules, which each have a particular shade. Molecules of some shades are attracted to the paper quickly, but others are not. That way, the inks split up into a variety of shades.

Fizzy fun

The bubbles of gas in soft drinks are carbon dioxide. You can mix up a powder and add it to ordinary drinks to make them bubble with carbon dioxide. You can also eat the powder to create a strange fizzing sensation on your tongue.

Bubbly drink

1. Put six teaspoons of citric acid crystals and three teaspoons of baking soda into the bowl.

2. With the back of the spoon, grind the two substances against the side of the bowl to make a fine powder.

3. Stir in two tablespoons of powdered sugar. Then pour the mixture into the clean, dry jar. Label it "Fizz powder".

4. To make a bubbling drink, put two spoons of fizz powder in the glass and fill it up with the ordinary drink. (Put the lid on the powder to keep it fresh.)

What happens?

The citric acid crystals dissolve in the liquid, so that tiny particles of it are floating. Because the citric acid is wet, it reacts with the baking soda to make carbon dioxide gas. The gas creates bubbles throughout the drink. The sugar in the fizz powder and the drink itself takes away the sour taste of the citric acid and the baking soda.

When the reaction is over there is no more carbon dioxide so eventually the drink goes flat.

Citrus fizz powder

To make a tongue-tingling powder, follow steps 1-3 from the instructions above, but add four tablespoons of sugar instead of two. Then spoon a little of the ground-up powder onto your tongue.

What happens?

When you lick the fizz powder, the citric acid crystals dissolve and react with the baking soda to make carbon dioxide gas. The fizz you feel on your tongue is the bubbles of gas.

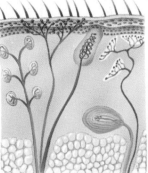

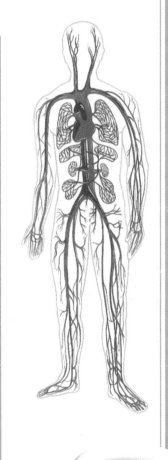

TESTING
YOUR BODY

You have five senses – seeing, hearing, smelling, touching and tasting. It can be fun to test them to see how they work and when they work best. You can also perform scientific tricks to fool your senses into giving the wrong answers.

You can do lots of other safe and simple tests on your body. For instance, you can do experiments to find out how your muscles work, how quickly your heart beats, how big your lungs are and how your voice works.

Tasting tests

These experiments investigate your sense of taste. For some of them you will need a friend to help you. Be prepared for some unexpected results.

Make a tongue map

Your tongue can detect four basic tastes: salty, sour, sweet and bitter. Try this test to discover where on your tongue each taste is strongest. Before you start, draw a tongue map like the one on the right so you can fill in your results.

> ### You will need
> - Small cup of black coffee
> - Small cup of salty water
> - Small cup of sugary water
> - Small cup of vinegar
> - Teaspoon • Pencil
> - 2 drinking straws
> - Slice of bread
> - Piece of paper

Your tongue map should look like this.

Drinking straw dropper
Vinegar

Release finger.
Drop of liquid

1. Cut two straws in half to make a dropper for each liquid. Dip a dropper into some vinegar, then cover the top with your finger to hold in the liquid.

2. Release a couple of drops of liquid onto each area of your tongue shown on the map above. Dry your tongue with bread between each test.

3. Mark where the vinegar tastes strongest. Rinse your mouth with fresh water then do the test with the other liquids. What results do you get?

What happens?

You taste sweet things most at the front of your tongue. Bitter things are sensed at the back, sour things on both sides and salty things are noticed right at the tip.

It's a fact!

Children have about 10,000 taste buds but some stop working as you get older, so tastes become less strong.

No nose surprise

> ### You will need
> - Grated apple • Grated carrot • Grated potato
> - 3 bowls • Blindfold
> - Spoon

1. Put some grated apple, carrot and potato into different bowls. Then blindfold yourself and hold your nose.

2. Ask a friend to feed you a spoonful of each food, one at a time. Can you recognize which food you are tasting?

Apple
Carrot
Potato

What happens?

When you eat, the smell of the food travels into your nose so you taste and smell at the same time. Your nose is much more sensitive than your tongue, so it can tell things apart much more accurately. Your tongue can only tell you that things taste sweet, sour, salty or bitter. Without your nose you cannot identify things in any more detail.

Funny looking food

The appearance of food helps you to guess how it will taste before you eat it. To see what happens when you change the way it looks, start by making the fast food shown here. You may want a grown-up to help you prepare the meal.

Murky milk

To change the look of milk, simply pour it into a glass containing several drops of blue food dye. The dye will not change the taste of the milk.

Blue burger

Dab food dye onto the white meat before you cook it. The result will look as strange as the blue burger shown in the picture below.

You could garnish your meal with tomatoes painted with red and blue dye.

Freaky fries

Drop uncooked french fries into 175ml (¼ pint) of water mixed with two tablespoons full of food dye for 30 minutes or so. Then dry them and cook them.

Give the freshly cooked food to someone you know for their meal. Don't let them see it before it is time to eat. What is their reaction to the food?

What happens?

If food looks strange, you expect it will taste different from usual. This reaction helps to keep you healthy because food sometimes changes its appearance when it goes bad.

INSTANT EXPERT

How does your tongue taste food?

Your tongue is covered with tiny taste feelers called taste buds. Chemicals in food and the air dissolve in saliva (spit) in your mouth. Taste signals travel along nerves to your brain.

How does your nose smell food?

Tiny drops of chemicals are given off by foods. They are carried in the air to the smell detectors in your nose. Smell signals travel to your brain in the same way as taste signals.

Sound experiments

Have you ever wondered how you hear things? On these two pages you can investigate how sounds reach your ears. You can also find out more about sounds and how they travel. You will need a friend to help with some of the experiments.

Watch sound travel

Normally you cannot see sounds moving at all. But by doing this experiment you can see evidence of sounds moving through the air.

You will need
• Plastic bottle • Plastic bag • Rubber band
• Scissors • Small candle

  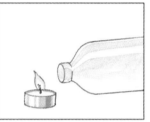 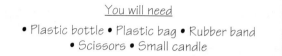

1. Cut the base off the plastic bottle. Then cut a piece from the plastic bag to cover the end of the bottle.

2. Stretch the piece of plastic tightly over the end of the bottle. Secure it with the rubber band.

3. Light the candle. Then hold the bottle with its neck about 2.5cm (1in) away from the candle.

4. Now tap the piece of plastic sharply with your fingertips. What happens to the flame?

What happens?

When you tap the piece of plastic you make tiny particles in the air beside it vibrate. These vibrating particles make the particles beside them vibrate too. The vibrations travel through the bottle and disturb the flame.

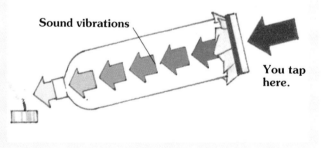

Sound vibrations

You tap here.

It's a fact!

Outer space is completely silent. This is because there is no air to carry the sounds.

INSTANT EXPERT

How do your ears work?

Sound vibrations travel down a tube, called the ear canal, inside your ear. They hit a thin sheet of skin at the end of your ear canal, called your eardrum, and make it vibrate.

Vibrations from your eardrum become stronger in your middle ear and are passed to your inner ear. In your inner ear the vibrations are changed into electrical messages. Nerves carry the messages to your brain, which tells you what you are hearing.

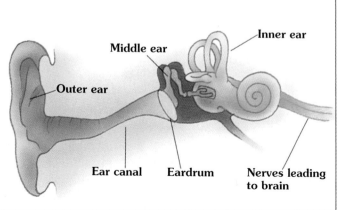

Middle ear · Inner ear · Outer ear · Ear canal · Eardrum · Nerves leading to brain

Sound through a tube

You will need
- Long tube made from cardboard or rolled-up paper • A watch

1. Hold the watch by your ear and move it away until you cannot hear it ticking. How far do you have to move it?

2. Cover the watch face with the tube and hold the other end against your ear. Now can you hear anything?

What happens?

Sound vibrations need energy to travel. As they spread out, they lose energy. That is why the sound from the watch doesn't reach you once it has moved away. When sound vibrations are trapped in the tube the energy does not spread out. So the ticking sound travels to the end of the tube.

Where's the sound?

You will need
- Jelly jar half-filled with dried beans
- Blindfold

1. Sit on a chair, blindfolded. Ask a friend to rattle the jar containing dried beans in different places behind you.

2. Say where you think the sound is coming from. How many times did you get it right?

What happens?

You have two ears so your brain can compare noise levels reaching each ear and calculate where a sound is coming from. When a sound is equally distant from both ears, it is hard to judge where it is being made.

It's a fact!

When a train moves at high speed the sound of the wheels on the track travels very quickly through the metal track itself. You can hear this as a hissing sound.

Speaking string

This experiment shows that sounds can travel through something solid.

You will need
- Piece of string at least 10m (33ft) long • 2 plastic cups

1. Make a small hole in the bottom of each cup. Push one end of the string through each hole and tie a knot in it.

2. Pull the string tight between the cups, with you at one end and a friend at the other. Make sure that it isn't touching anything else.

3. Take turns for one of you to hold your cup to your ear while the other whispers into their cup. Can you hear each other?

What happens?

Your voice can be heard far away because it travels along the string, which is solid. Sounds travel better and faster along solids than they do through the air. Test this by tapping very gently on a table top. Then put your ear against the table and tap again.

How your eyes work

Your eyes work in a similar way to cameras. By following the instructions below you can make a simple camera out of a yogurt pot and some tracing paper.

Making a simple camera

Black paint reduces reflections inside the pot.

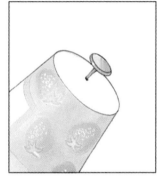

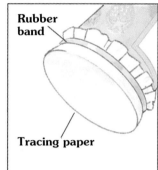

Rubber band

Tracing paper

Hold the yogurt pot viewer level with your eyes.

1. Paint the inside of a yogurt pot with black poster paint. If you mix a drop of dishwashing liquid with the paint, it will stick better.

2. When the paint is thoroughly dry, push the tack into the base of the yogurt pot to make a small pinhole. Then ease the tack out carefully.

3. Stretch a piece of tracing paper tightly over the top of the pot and secure it with the rubber band. This is the viewing screen of your camera.

4. Light a small candle, make the room dark and point the base of the pot at the candle, from about 50cm (20in) away. What do you see on the screen?

What happens?

Some light from the flame travels through the pinhole and lands on the paper screen. The light rays travel in straight lines. When they go through the pinhole the rays from the top of the candle hit the bottom part of the screen and rays from the bottom of the candle hit the top of the screen. So the image is upside down.

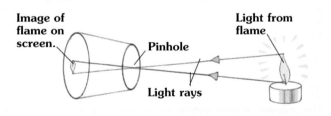

Image of flame on screen.

Light from flame

Pinhole

Light rays

INSTANT EXPERT

What happens inside your eyes?

Light travels through a hole at the front of your eye, called the pupil. It lands on a screen called the retina, making an upside-down image. A nerve, called the optic nerve, joins your retina to your brain. Your brain turns the image the right way up and tells you what you are seeing.

Object

Image on retina.

Pupil

Optic nerve leads to brain.

Light rays

How does a real camera work?

Real cameras have light-sensitive film at the back instead of a screen. When you press a button, a shutter lets light in. The light marks a picture on the film. This is printed on paper to a make a photograph.

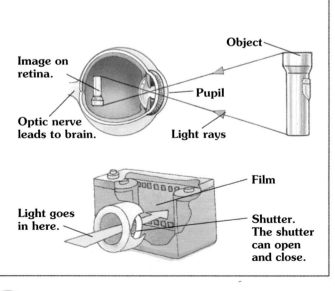

Film

Light goes in here.

Shutter. The shutter can open and close.

Eye tests

Your eyes are constantly adjusting so you have a clear view of the things around you. Try the tests below to find out how they adapt to different conditions.

Growing pupils

Stand in a dim room for a few minutes then look at your eyes in a mirror. Look closely at your pupils. Then put the light on. What happens to your pupils?

What happens?

In bright light pupils close up to stop too much light from damaging your eyes.

However, in dim light pupils open up to let more light in so you can see more.

One eye teaser

This experiment shows why you need two eyes to judge exactly where things are.

> You will need
> • Pen with a lid

Close one eye, then hold up a pen in one hand and its top in the other. With your arms slightly bent, try to put the top on the pen. Can you tell if the top is in front or behind the pen? Now try using both eyes.

Seeing in the dark

> You will need
> • Crayons in different shades

Take some crayons into an unlit room. You can see a little after a while because there is always some light. Look at the crayons. Can you tell them apart?

What happens?

You can see the shapes of the crayons but it is difficult to tell which shade is which. The parts of your eyes that identify different shades (called cones) need a lot of light in order to work properly.

It's a fact!

The biggest animal in the world also has the biggest eyes. It is the blue whale. Each of its eyes are as big as a soccer ball - about 23cm (9in) across.

Bright light. Pupils are very small.   **Dim light. Pupils are very large.**

What happens?

Your two eyes give you two slightly different views. Your brain compares these two views to judge exactly where things are.

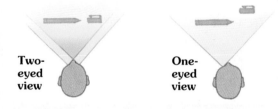

Two-eyed view   **One-eyed view**

When you close one eye, you have only one view, so it is much harder for your brain to judge the distance between objects.

It's a fact!

Eagles have the best eyesight of all animals, so they can see their prey from very high in the sky. An eagle can spot a hare from about 3km (2 miles) away.

Eye tricks

Your eyes can deceive you and see something that is not really there. This is called an optical illusion. In the picture on the right, for example, the ladders are the same length although the lines around them make them look as if they are different sizes.

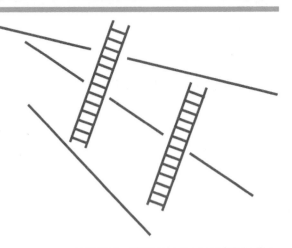

Straight lines?

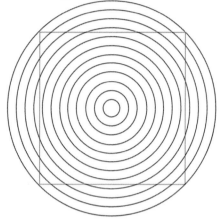

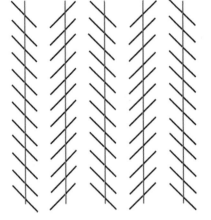

What happens?

In all these tests your eyes are fooled by the black lines, which make the red ones seem as if they are either curved or leaning.

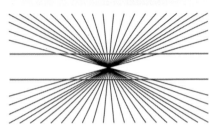

Look at the picture above. Are the red lines straight?

In this picture, are the red lines absolutely parallel?

Look hard at this picture. Are the two red lines straight?

Longer or shorter?

Try the tests below then use a ruler to find out if your answers are right.

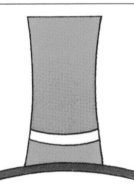

Which is longer, the top red line or the lower one?

Is this strange looking hat as tall as the brim is wide?

What happens?

When you look at the pictures, your eyes are confused by the lines. In each trick, the lines are the same length.

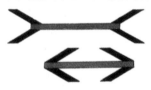

Are these two red lines the same length?

Floating finger

Hold one finger from each hand up in front of your eyes. Stare hard at something beyond your fingers, while keeping them in place. Do not look directly at your fingers though.

You should see something unexpected appear in front of your eyes. But what is it?

What happens?

Because you are looking beyond your fingers, each eye sees both fingers at once, making four in all. The two extra fingers overlap to make a small floating finger.

Hole in your hand

<u>You will need</u>
• Sheet of stiff paper 30 x 20cm (12 x 8in) • Adhesive tape

What happens?

One eye is looking down the tube and the other is looking at your hand. The two views mix together so you see a hand with a hole in it.

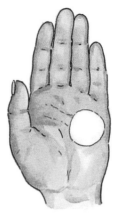

1. Make a tube by rolling up the sheet of stiff paper. Tape the edge so the tube holds together.

2. Hold the tube up to your right eye. Hold your left hand up beside the tube.

3. Stare hard down the tube, keeping your left eye open. Do you see a hole in your hand?

Which is bigger?

Look at these two circles. Which one of them do you think is the biggest?

What happens?

The light blue circle looks bigger because light, bright shades seem to be larger than dark, dull ones.

Find your blind spot

Hold this page at arm's length. Close your left eye and stare hard at the square with your right one. Slowly bring the page closer to your face. Does the green spot disappear? Now close your right eye and try again, looking at the green spot instead.

What happens?

Each of your eyes has a blind spot, where the optic nerve (the nerve that carries picture messages to your brain) joins onto the back of your retina (your eye's viewing screen). In this test, the square or circle disappears when it is in line with your blind spot because there are no sight sensors (called rods and cones) there.

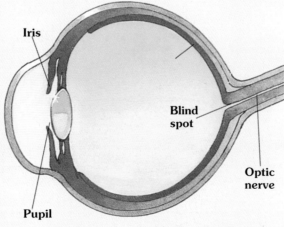

Iris

Blind spot

Optic nerve

Pupil

It's a fact!

Eating carrots helps you to see. They contain a substance called carotene, which helps your eyes to stay healthy.

Work your muscles

Did you know that your heart is made of muscle? It squeezes over and over again to pump blood around your body. Try the tests below to find out how hard it works. Then try the projects on the opposite page to discover more about other muscles in your body.

Pumping blood

Your heart is a muscular bag inside your chest. Each time it beats it fills with blood and squeezes it out through blood vessels that go all over your body. Try this test to discover how quickly your heart beats.

1. Hold two fingers on your wrist as shown. Can you feel a regular throbbing? It is called your pulse. Your fingers are feeling a blood vessel near the surface.

2. Flatten a small ball of playdough and stand the toothpick in the middle.

3. Relax your arm and rest your hand on a table. Balance the playdough on your wrist where you can feel your pulse. Can you see the toothpick move?

4. The toothpick moves each time your heart beats and pushes blood through the blood vessel. Count how many times it moves in 30 seconds.

5. Walk very quickly for two minutes. Balance the playdough on your wrist again. Now how many times does the toothpick move in 30 seconds?

You will need
- Playdough • Toothpick
- Watch that shows seconds

It's a fact!

Your heart beats about once every second. This means that it pumps about 100,000 times a day throughout your whole life. Your heart is made of a special type of muscle called cardiac muscle. Unlike your other muscles, it never gets tired and never stops working until you die.

What happens?

The toothpick should move much more quickly after you have exercised. When you exercise, your heart beats faster to send blood around your body more quickly. It does this so that the blood can take oxygen (which it gets from the air you breathe) to your muscles. It also carries dissolved food.

Muscles use oxygen and food to make energy.

Squeezing hard

Your heart is about the size of your fist. Try this test to find out how strong it is.

Squeeze a tennis ball as hard as you can in one hand. Can you squash it?

What happens?

You may find it hard to squash the tennis ball, but your heart squeezes with enough force to squash the ball every time it beats.

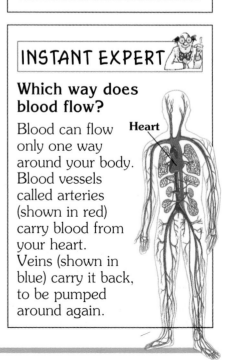

INSTANT EXPERT

Which way does blood flow?

Blood can flow only one way around your body. Blood vessels called arteries (shown in red) carry blood from your heart. Veins (shown in blue) carry it back, to be pumped around again.

Heart

Make a model arm

Many of your muscles work in pairs – like the strings on this model arm.

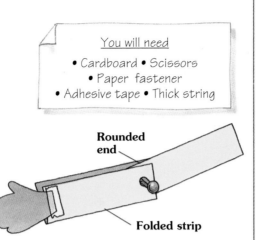

You will need
• Cardboard • Scissors
• Paper fastener
• Adhesive tape • Thick string

Rounded end

Folded strip

1. Cut two strips of cardboard, one twice as wide as the other. Fold the wide strip in half along its width. Give the narrow strip one rounded end.

2. Put the rounded end of the narrow strip in the fold of the other strip and join them with the paper fastener. Tape a hand shape at the other end.

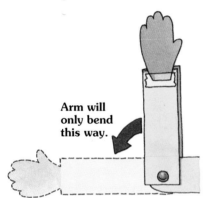

Arm will only bend this way.

3. Try bending the model arm. If the paper strips have been joined correctly it should be able to bend only up and down, just like your own arm.

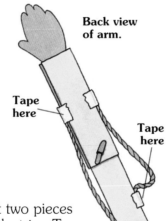

Back view of arm.

Tape here

Tape here

4. Cut two pieces of thick string. Tape a piece to each side of your model arm, as shown here.

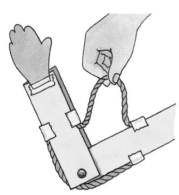

5. When you have finished making the arm, pull one of the strings then the other. The arm should move. Can you see that it is similar to your own arm?

What happens?

The string on top of the model arm makes it bend. The string underneath makes it straighten.

The model works in the same way as the muscles in your own arm.

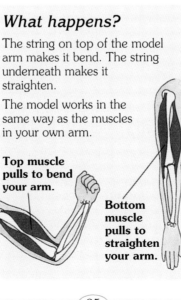

Top muscle pulls to bend your arm.

Bottom muscle pulls to straighten your arm.

Muscle strength

The more you use your muscles, the stonger they become – as this test proves.

1. Ask a friend to press his hands tightly together. Try to pull them apart by gripping each wrist and pulling them to the sides.

You will find it very difficult to pull your friend's hands apart in this position because the muscles you are pulling with are not used very often.

2. Try the same test again but this time cross your hands over and push your friend's hands apart.

It is easier to move your friend's hands apart because you are using different muscles. These pushing muscles are often used so they are strong.

INSTANT EXPERT

How many muscles do you have?

There are over 600 muscles in your body. The biggest are the gluteus maximus muscles in your buttocks and thighs. The smallest are the stapedius muscles inside your ears. They are less than 1.25mm ($^1/_{20}$in) long.

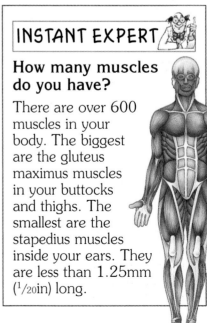

More body tests

Each time you breathe your lungs fill with air and empty again. As the air flows up through your throat it can make the sounds of your voice. Follow the projects on these pages to discover more about how your lungs and voice work.

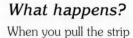

It's a fact!

There are about 96,000km (59,520 miles) of blood vessels (tubes that carry blood) in your body. This is enough to stretch more than twice around the Earth's middle.

Breathing model

You will need
• Clear plastic bottle • Balloon • Plastic bag
• Adhesive tape • Scissors • Small strip of thick paper

1. Using the scissors, carefully cut the plastic bottle in half. Then stretch a balloon over the neck, and push it inside.

2. Stretch a piece of plastic bag over the open end of the half bottle. Tape it all around so that there are no gaps.

3. Tape a strip of thick paper to the middle of the plastic. Pull on the paper strip and then push it. What happens to the balloon?

What happens?

When you pull the strip down, the space around the balloon gets bigger. Air moves into the balloon to fill the space. The opposite happens when you push the strip. Your chest works in a very similar way when you breathe in and out.

Pull the strip.   **Push the strip.**

Test your lungs

You will need
• Clear plastic bottle with a lid
• Bowl of water
• Flexible drinking straw

Have you ever wondered just how much air your lungs can hold? Try this simple test to find out.

Fill the plastic bottle with water. Put on the lid. Hold it in a bowl of water and take off the lid.

Don't let in any air.

Put the straw into the bottle. Breathe in. Blow into the straw until you can't breathe out any more. What happens?

Don't let the straw come out.

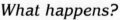  

What happens?

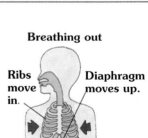

A space forms at the top of the bottle. This shows how much air you were able to hold in your lungs in one breath.

INSTANT EXPERT

How do lungs work?

When you breathe in, a muscle under your chest, called your diaphragm, moves down and your ribs move out. This makes the space in your chest bigger and pulls air into your lungs. When you breathe out your diaphragm moves up and your ribs go in to push the air out.

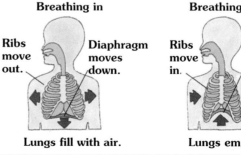

Breathing in

Ribs move out.   Diaphragm moves down.

Lungs fill with air.

Breathing out

Ribs move in.   Diaphragm moves up.

Lungs empty.

Feel your voice

Place two fingers on the front of your throat, just below your chin. Can you feel a hard lump? Inside the lump are two stretchy flaps of skin called your vocal cords. With your fingers on them, try talking. Can you feel anything happening to your vocal cords?

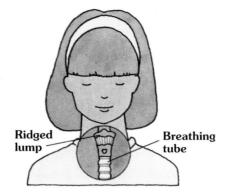

Ridged lump

Breathing tube

Balloon voice

Using a balloon, you can find out how your vocal cords make sounds.

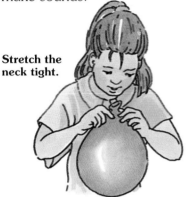

Stretch the neck tight.

1. Blow up the balloon. Stretch its neck tightly as you let the air out. What sound does it make as the air escapes?

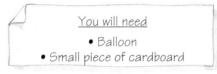

You will need
• Balloon
• Small piece of cardboard

Cardboard tube

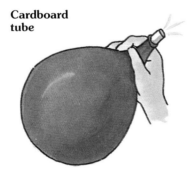

2. Make a thin cardboard tube. Blow up the balloon again and put the tube in its neck. Does the air make a sound as it rushes out?

Seeing vibrations

Try this experiment to see how your vocal cords make different sounds.

1. Stretch the rubber band between your hands and pluck it with your thumb.

You will need
• Rubber band

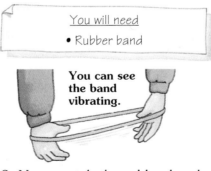

You can see the band vibrating.

2. Now stretch the rubber band more tightly. Has the sound changed in any way?

What happens?

When the band is stretched gently it vibrates and makes low notes. When it is stretched more tightly it makes higher notes when it vibrates. Your vocal cords make different sounds in the same way.

What happens?

The vocal cords vibrate as air from your lungs flows past them. This makes the sound of your voice.

If you could see down your throat, your vocal cords would look a little like this.

It's a fact!

Bush crickets don't have vocal cords. They make a singing noise by rubbing their wings together to make them vibrate.

What happens?

Muscles in your throat stretch your vocal cords, like the neck of the balloon. When the cords are stretched, they vibrate as air flows past them, and make a noise. When they are relaxed (like the balloon with the tube in its neck) they don't vibrate – so they do not make a noise.

INSTANT EXPERT

Why do you breathe?

You need to breathe to take oxygen from the air into your body. Your cells (the tiny pieces that make up your body) use oxygen to release energy from food. Without oxygen they would die in a few minutes. Your cells also make a waste gas called carbon dioxide, which you breathe out. Oxygen and carbon dioxide are carried between your cells and lungs by your blood.

Touch tests

Whenever you touch something, tiny nerve endings near the surface of your skin send messages to your brain. Try the tests below to find out more about your sense of touch and discover where it is strongest.

How many pencils?

You will need
• Two pencils

1. Close your eyes. Then ask a friend to touch you very lightly in all the places shown on this picture, using sometimes one pencil and sometimes two.

2. Say when you feel two points and when you feel only one. Do you get the correct number every time you are touched?

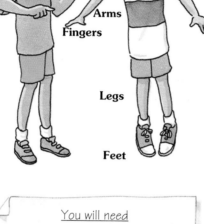

The two pencils must be held close together.

Lips

Back

Arms

Fingers

Legs

Feet

What happens?

Probably, you will not be correct every time. You will be correct most often in the places where your nerve endings are close together, such as in your fingers and lips. In other areas, such as your back, the nerve endings are too far apart to feel both points.

In this picture, the parts of the upper body with most nerve endings have been enlarged.

Cold touch

1. Put lots of ice cubes in a bowl and sprinkle a few grains of rice alongside the bowl.

2. Hold one hand in the bowl of ice cubes. Count to 30 slowly.

3. Dry your hand and try to pick up some grains of rice.

You will need
• Bowl • Ice cubes • Rice

What happens?

It is hard to pick up the rice because your sense of touch doesn't work as well when your skin is cold.

INSTANT EXPERT

How does skin feel different sensations?

Different types of nerve endings pick up different feelings, such as heat, cold, touch, pressure, pleasure and pain.

Nerve endings

This diagram shows inside your skin.

ELECTRICITY AND MAGNETS

How does a magnet work? How does electricity flow? In this section you can find the answers. You can also see how to make magnets of your own, and a battery, plus magnetic compasses that help you to find out where you are in the world. There's also an electrical game and a working model of an electric motor to build.

⚠️

One important word of warning though – never use electricity from an electrical socket for these experiments. It is far too strong and can give serious electric shocks or even kill you.

Magnet tests

Magnets are things that can pull (attract) certain metals to them, especially iron and steel. Magnets are usually metals themselves, and you can use them to pass on magnetism to other metals. You can buy magnets cheaply in all shapes and sizes – a selection is shown on the right.

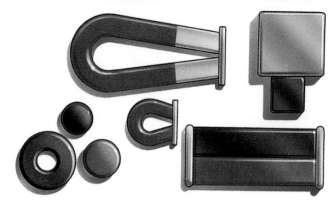

Magnetism travels through things

You will need
- Magnet • Glass of water • Paper clip
- Cardboard • Wooden or plastic ruler

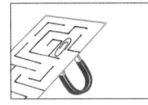  

Draw a maze on some cardboard. Put the paper clip on the maze. Can you guide it through the maze, using a magnet underneath?

Drop the paper clip into the glass of water. Can you rescue the paper clip without wetting either your hand or the magnet?

Can you get the paper clip to climb the ruler without touching it with your hands? The picture should give you a clue how to do it.

What happens?

Because magnetic forces travel through most things that cannot be magnetized the magnet is able to attract the paper clip. Plastic, wood, cardboard, glass and water are all things that cannot be magnetized.

Making a magnet

You will need
- Strong bar magnet
- Steel needle

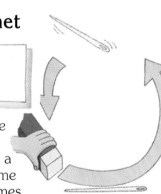

Stroke the steel needle from one end to the other with one end of a bar magnet, in the same direction, about 40 times.

What happens?

The metal inside the needle is made up of tiny parts, called domains. Each domain is like a mini-magnet. However, they point in different directions and cancel each other out.

When you stroke the magnet over the needle, it causes the domains in the needle to all point the same way. So the needle becomes magnetized.

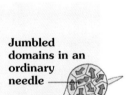

Jumbled domains in an ordinary needle

Ordered domains in a magnetized needle

INSTANT EXPERT

Can a magnet lose its power?

Yes. If the domains of the magnet are disturbed the magnet will lose its power. One way to make a magnet lose its power is by dropping it on the floor lots of times. Every time you drop it on the floor the domains are shaken. Eventually they become out of line, so the magnetism is lost. You could try this with a magnetized needle.

The more a magnetized object is dropped, the more it loses its magnetism.

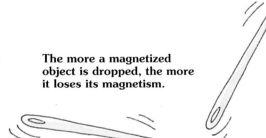

Floating magnets

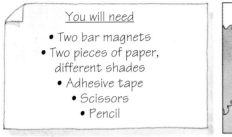

Do not hold this magnet.

Magnets will behave in one of two ways if you point one at another. You can use this to make a magnet float in the air, following the instructions here.

1. Push the end of one magnet to the end of the other. They will either pull together or push apart. If they push, turn one around so they pull together.

2. Cut out and tape shaded paper on the ends (called the poles) that pull together. Use one shade for one magnet, and a different shade for the other.

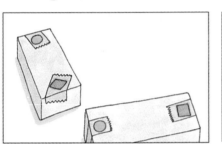

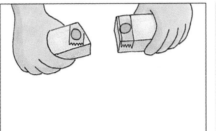

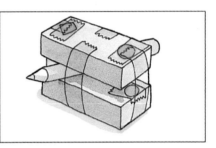

3. Turn both magnets around and repeat step 2. Mark them with pieces of the same paper that you used in step 2, so that all ends have paper on them.

4. Try to push two of the same-shaded poles together. You should be able to feel them pushing against one another, refusing to stick together.

5. Copying the picture above, tape the two magnets together with a pencil between them. What happens when you remove the pencil?

Try pressing down on the top magnet. It should spring up again when you stop pressing it.

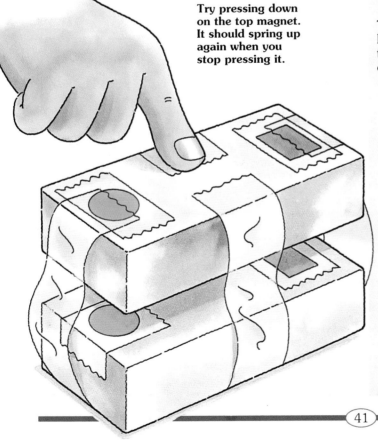

What happens?

The magnet on top will float over the one beneath it. Each magnet has two kinds of pole. One is called north, the other is south. Poles of the same kind push each other away but different poles pull each other together.

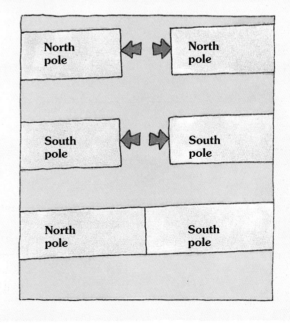

North pole		North pole
South pole		South pole
North pole		South pole

More magnet tests

Did you know that the Earth acts like a giant magnet? It causes other magnets to point to the top of the Earth, called the north. You can do experiments that prove this, using a bar magnet. It will always come to rest pointing the same way, time after time.

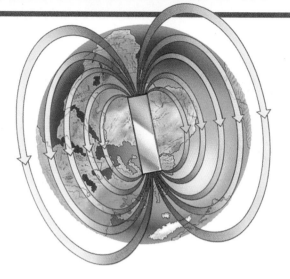

Free-floating magnet

You will need
- Small pieces of paper • Small plastic bowl • Water
- Adhesive tape • Large bowl • Bar magnet • Pen

Mark the large bowl opposite the magnet's ends with pieces of paper.

1. Secure the bar magnet in the middle of the small plastic bowl, using adhesive tape as shown in the picture above.

2. Float the small bowl in the large bowl filled with water. When the small bowl stops, repeat the test. What happens?

Making a compass

A compass is an instrument used for finding directions. It is made of a magnetic needle which floats in liquid. You can make a simple compass of your own fairly easily.

You will need
- Piece of thin cardboard
- The free-floating magnet from above
- Scissors

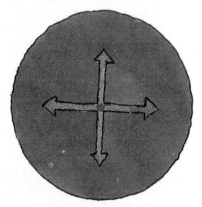

To check which end of the magnet is pointing north, see the top of the next page.

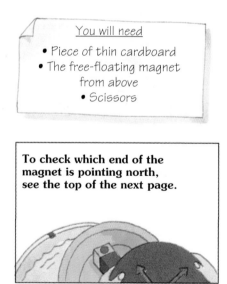

1. Cut a circle of cardboard to fit the small bowl. Then mark east, west, north and south on the cardboard, as shown here.

2. Place the cardboard in the small bowl so that "N" is over the north end of the magnet. Once the magnet has stopped moving all the arrows will point in the right directions.

What happens?

No matter how often you move the small bowl, it will always stop with the magnet pointing the same way. The Earth's magnetic force causes the magnet to stop with one end pointing to the top of the Earth (the North Pole) and the other end pointing to the bottom (the South Pole).

INSTANT EXPERT

Why is the Earth magnetic?

At the very middle of the Earth is a hot solid lump, made up of two metals - iron and nickel. It is surrounded by a liquid made of molten iron and nickel.

As the Earth goes around, the molten layer moves around very slowly. Scientists think that this makes the Earth magnetic.

Earth's core

It's a fact!

The Ancient Chinese invented the first compasses around two thousand years ago.

Checking for north and south

Go outside at noon on a sunny day. If you live in the northern part of the world (see the map on the right to check which part you live in) your shadow will point to the north. If you live in the southern part of the world your shadow will point to the south.

NORTH

EQUATOR

SOUTH

Magnetic forces

You will need
- Magnet (any type will do)
- Thin piece of plastic or cardboard • Iron filings (available at a pharmacy)

Magnetic forces work all around a magnet, not just at its ends. By following this experiment you can see how the forces work.

Put a magnet under some thin plastic or cardboard. Gradually sprinkle some iron filings on top. What happens?

The iron filings collect around the two open ends of a horseshoe magnet. Farther down the magnet, away from the ends, the magnetism is weaker.

It's a fact!

Some animals, such as the arctic tern, are thought to be sensitive to the Earth's magnetism. Scientists think they use it to help them find their way.

On a bar magnet the magnetism is strongest at the ends, so lots of iron filings are pulled to them.

What happens?

The magnetic forces work in a regular pattern all around the magnet. The iron filings become magnetized and collect together at the places where magnetic forces are working most strongly. They line up showing the direction of the force.

Because the magnetic forces work all around the magnet, the iron filings stand up at different angles, depending on which forces around the magnet are working on them.

This diagram shows how the magnetic forces work around a magnet.

The space where the magnetic forces work is called the magnetic field.

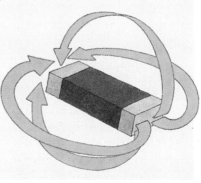

Static electricity

Electricity is always trying to move from one thing to another. If it cannot move for some reason, it is called static electricity. There are several ways that you can create static electricity, and see its effects. These experiments are most successful if you do them on a dry day.

Sticky balloon

You can use the forces of static electricity to make a balloon stick to your clothing or hair. It's best to wear something made of wool if you want the balloon to stick to your clothes.

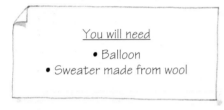

> You will need
> • Balloon
> • Sweater made from wool

1. Blow up the balloon. Rub it vigorously against your sweater or your hair, about ten times.

2. Hold it to your hair or sweater for a moment and then let go. Does the balloon move?

What happens?

When you rub the sweater with the balloon, each one takes a different electrical charge (see page 45). The balloon becomes negatively charged, and the sweater becomes positively charged. These opposites attract each other.

Before rubbing

The positive and negative charges are balanced in both things.

After rubbing

The balloon borrows some of the sweater's negative charge.

Pushing apart

> You will need
> • Two balloons
> • Two pieces of nylon thread, the same length
> • Adhesive tape
> • A piece of cloth made from wool (a wool scarf is ideal)

1. Take the lengths of nylon thread and tape them to the top of a door frame, spacing them about 2.5cm (1in) apart. Tie a balloon to the end of each thread, so they are hanging at the same height. They should be touching.

2. Rub the balloons with the cloth to give them an electrical charge, one at a time. Let go of the balloons. How do they hang now?

What happens?

Things that are made of the same material always take the same charge. Balloons become negatively charged when you rub them. Matching charges of static electricity always push each other away, like matching poles of a magnet, so the balloons hang a little distance apart.

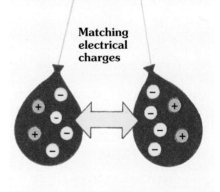

Matching electrical charges

INSTANT EXPERT

What gives a thing an electrical charge?

Everything is made up of atoms. Atoms contain lots of little particles, called protons and electrons, which have electrical charges. Protons always have a positive (+) electrical charge. Electrons always have a negative (–) electrical charge. Electrons are much lighter than protons. They move around, but protons always stay still.

Normally, atoms have the same number of protons and electrons so the charges cancel each other out. Sometimes, the electrons jump from one thing to another (like in the experiments on these two pages). The atom that gets extra electrons becomes negatively charged. The one that loses electrons becomes positively charged.

Protons (+) stay in the middle of the atom, called the nucleus. In this picture they are shown in red.

Electrons (–) whizz around the edge of the atom. They can move from one atom to another.

Miniature lightning

This experiment is really effective if you do it in a darkened room. It may make your fingers tingle a bit!

> **You will need**
> • Large baking tray
> • Playdough
> • Large plastic bag
> • Metal lid from a jar, or a coin

It's a fact!

Lightning can travel at a top speed of around 160,000km (100,000miles) per second.

1. Press down a large lump of playdough in the middle of the baking tray. Press it down hard to make sure it is firmly stuck to the tray.

2. Put the tray down on the plastic bag. Hold the playdough and rub the tray around and around on the bag for about 30 seconds or so.

3. Holding the playdough only, pick up the tray. Hold the metal lid (or coin) close to one corner. Can you see a spark jump from the tray to the lid?

What happens?

Rubbing the tray on the bag gives the tray a negative charge. When you hold the metal lid near it, the charge jumps from the tray to the lid. You see a flash as the charge travels through the air.

Lightning works in a similar way. The bottom of a thunder cloud develops a negative charge. This creates a positive charge in the ground below. When the charge is strong enough, the air cannot stop the charge from jumping from the cloud to the ground – and you see a flash of lightning.

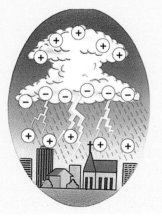

It's a fact!

Thunder is the sound created by a flash of lightning.

Making connections

Electricity will always flow from one thing to another if it possibly can, forming an electrical current. But it can only flow through things that will allow it to move. You can do experiments to find out which things allow electricity to pass through them (called conductors) and which things do not (called insulators).

Light the lamp

For an electrical current to flow from a battery there must be a way for the electricity to flow from one terminal to the other. This is called an electrical circuit. In this experiment, the circuit has a gap. Find out which objects will complete the circuit and light the bulb.

> ### You will need
>
> • 4.5 volt battery • Insulated wire
> • Small light bulb held in a bulb holder
> • Adhesive tape
> • Things to test: foil, glass, paper clip, plastic, coin, rubber band, pencil

1. Set up the battery, bulb and three wires as shown in the picture on the right.

2. Touch the free ends of the wires onto each of the things to be tested. Which ones make the bulb light up?

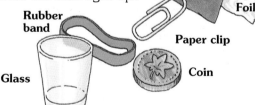

Rubber band

Plastic

Foil

Paper clip

Glass

Coin

IMPORTANT WARNING

Never use electricity from a socket for this experiment. It is far too strong and can give serious electric shocks or even kill.

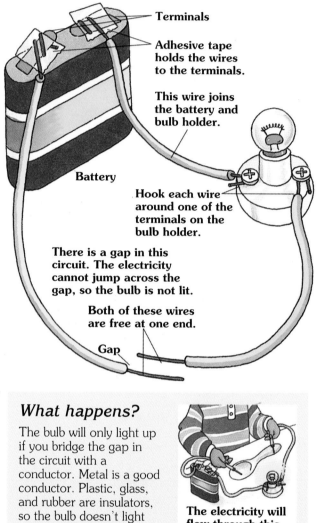

Terminals

Adhesive tape holds the wires to the terminals.

This wire joins the battery and bulb holder.

Battery

Hook each wire around one of the terminals on the bulb holder.

There is a gap in this circuit. The electricity cannot jump across the gap, so the bulb is not lit.

Both of these wires are free at one end.

Gap

What happens?

The bulb will only light up if you bridge the gap in the circuit with a conductor. Metal is a good conductor. Plastic, glass, and rubber are insulators, so the bulb doesn't light up when you hold the wires to them.

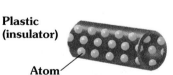

The electricity will flow through this metal spoon.

INSTANT EXPERT

How do things conduct electricity?

Inside atoms are tiny things called electrons, which carry an electric charge. When electrons flow together in one direction, they carry electricity with them.

Metal (conductor)

Electrons move

Atom

Things that conduct electricity, such as metals, have electrons that are free to move and carry electricity from place to place.

Plastic (insulator)

Atom

In insulators, such as plastic, the electrons are held tightly within the atoms and cannot move. So they cannot carry electricity from place to place.

Steady hand game

This game makes use of the fact that electricity will only flow around a complete circuit – and it will stop flowing the moment the circuit is broken. The idea of the game is to avoid connecting the circuit, so that you don't make the buzzer sound.

<u>You will need</u>
• 6 volt buzzer • 4.5 volt battery • Adhesive tape
• 1m (40in) florists' wire (or some other flexible wire without insulation) • Ballpoint pen • Shoe box
• 50cm (20in) insulated wire • Scissors

1. With the ballpoint pen, make three holes in the lid of the shoe box. Carefully strip 2.5cm (1in) of the covering off each end of some insulated wire.

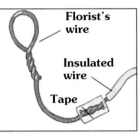

Florist's wire

Insulated wire

Tape

2. Cut 15cm (6in) off some florists' wire and bend one end into a loop. Twist the other end onto a bare end of the insulated wire, then tape them together.

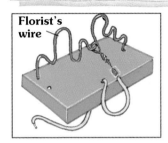

Florist's wire

3. Feed the other end of the insulated wire through the middle hole in the lid. Bend the rest of the florist's wire into a wiggly line. Thread the loop onto it.

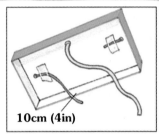

10cm (4in)

4. Push the ends of the wire through the holes at the ends of the box lid. Tape both ends to the lid's underside, leaving 10cm (4in) of one end hanging free.

Buzzer   Battery

5. Twist the long end of the wiggly wire to the free buzzer wire. Tape the insulated wire's bare end to one battery terminal. Tape the other terminal to the buzzer. Does the buzzer sound?

How to play

Start with the loop at one end of the wiggly wire. Holding the looped wire in one hand, move it to the other end of the wiggly wire without letting them touch. This can be hard to do.

If the buzzer doesn't sound when the wires touch, check for any loose connections. If there are no loose connections, check that your battery has not run down.

What happens?

If the wire loop and the wiggly wire touch, they complete the electrical circuit, which causes the buzzer to sound. If you keep the wires apart, the circuit stays broken, so the buzzer won't sound.

You could bend the wiggly wire into almost any shape you like. This one has been made into the shape of a shark.

Hide the buzzer and the battery inside the box.

You could decorate your box to match the shape you have chosen for the wire.

Making sparks

With a few simple things you can make a real battery which makes its own electricity. You can also build an electrical switch, which you use to turn an electrical supply on and off.

Build your own battery

This simple battery is called a voltaic pile. It looks nothing like a battery you put in an alarm clock or personal stereo but it works in just the same way.

You will need

• Copper coins (at least ten, all the same size) • Cup of water with 10 teaspoons of salt in it • Two pieces of insulated copper wire • Baking foil (or zinc washers) • Kitchen paper towels • Adhesive tape • Scissors

Cut out shapes using scissors or a sharp craft knife.

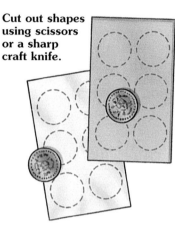

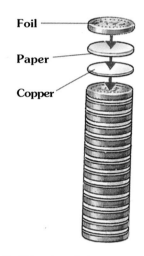

Foil
Paper
Copper

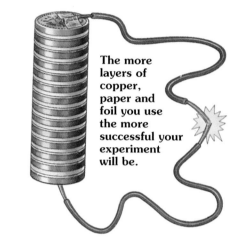

The more layers of copper, paper and foil you use the more successful your experiment will be.

1. From your stock of same-sized copper coins, take one and draw around it lots of times onto a sheet of baking foil and a paper towel. Cut out the shapes, then wet the paper disks with very salty water.

2. Pile the disks in groups of three – foil, paper, copper – one on top of the other until you have completed the pile. Each group of three disks makes one cell. The whole pile makes a battery.

3. Strip the ends of the pieces of insulated copper wire. Tape the end of one wire to the top of the pile. Tape the end of the other wire to the bottom. Touch the two ends together. In a dark room you should see a spark.

What happens?

The coins and foil react with the salt water to create electricity. This flows along the wires.

It's a fact!

The word electricity comes from the ancient Greek word *elektron*, meaning "amber".

INSTANT EXPERT

How does a battery work?

A common kind of battery (the kind you would put in a personal stereo) is called a dry cell. It contains a chemical paste which reacts to create an electrical charge. The charge is carried along a metal conductor.

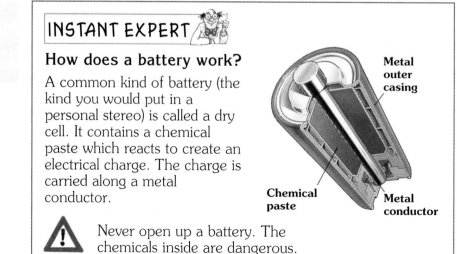

Metal outer casing

Chemical paste

Metal conductor

⚠ Never open up a battery. The chemicals inside are dangerous.

Make an electrical switch

Make this model of an electrical switch to see roughly what happens beneath the covers of things such as light switches and the switches on cassette players.

<u>You will need</u>
- 4.5 volt battery • Small bulb and bulb holder (available from electrical shops) • Paper clip • Adhesive tape
- 3 electrical wires with plastic coverings
- Small piece of cardboard • 2 paper fasteners

Make sure the paper clip can touch this fastener.

The legs must not touch.

1. Join the battery, bulb and three wires as shown in the picture above. Attach the wires to the battery using some adhesive tape.

2. Push one paper fastener through some cardboard. Hook a paper clip onto the second fastener and push this fastener through the cardboard.

3. Turn the cardboard over. Wrap one wire around each paper fastener. Bend the legs of the fasteners back and tape them down.

What happens?

When you press the paper clip against the paper fasteners, you are joining up an electrical circuit. This enables electricity to flow around the wires and through the light bulb. This makes the bulb light up. When you break the connection you stop the electricity from flowing so the light stops shining.

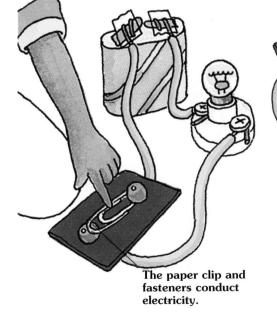

The paper clip and fasteners conduct electricity.

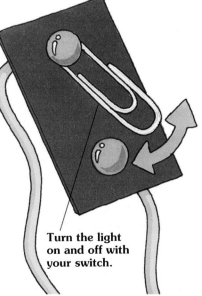

Turn the light on and off with your switch.

4. Take the paper clip and press it onto the free paper fastener. Electricity should flow around the circuit. What happens to the light bulb?

5. Now take the paper clip off the paper fastener. What happens to the light bulb this time? Why do you think this happens?

It's a fact!

Some fish, such as torpedo rays, make electricity in their bodies. They use it to stun other animals so they can catch them.

Electricity and magnets

When electricity starts to flow through a wire a magnetic field forms around it. You can test this by doing the experiment below. After, you could do the project that begins on the opposite page to see how you can combine electricity with magnets to make an electric motor.

Its a fact!

Magnets are used on certain types of train instead of wheels. Their force holds the train just above a special track (which is also magnetic) and push it along.

Make a magnetic wire

The electric current that flows through a straight wire has a fairly weak magnetic field. By coiling the wire you can make it much more magnetic.

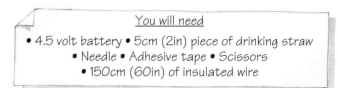

You will need
• 4.5 volt battery • 5cm (2in) piece of drinking straw
• Needle • Adhesive tape • Scissors
• 150cm (60in) of insulated wire

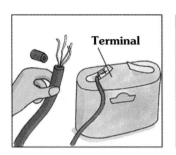

Terminal

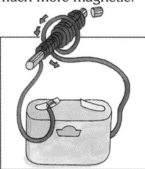

Electricity flows once the terminals are connected.

What happens?

Because the wire is coiled, the current that flows through it has a strong magnetic field. Its magnetism is powerful enough to attract the needle and make it float inside the straw.

This coil of wire is called a solenoid.

1. Cut off the plastic coating at each end of the insulated wire. Tape one end onto a terminal of the battery.

2. Wind the wire neatly onto the piece of drinking straw. Wind on three layers. Put a strip of tape on each layer to hold it.

3. Tape the free end of the wire onto the second terminal. Hold the needle lightly just inside the coil, then let go. What does it do?

Make an electromagnet

An electromagnet is a magnet that uses electricity to make it work. You can turn the solenoid you made in the last experiment into an electromagnet by putting a long iron or steel nail inside the straw.

You will need
• Equipment as for last experiment
• Large steel nail

Tape the nail in place if it is loose.

What happens?

When the electric current passes through the wire, the nail quickly becomes magnetized. The magnetic force is strong enough for the nail to pick up things.

When the current is broken an iron nail should lose its magnetism once more.

1. Place a nail inside the drinking straw. Check that the insulated wires are still taped to the battery.

2. Your nail should now be able to pick up other metal things, such as paper clips and pins.

3. Now take one end of the wire away from the battery to stop the current. Do things still stick to the nail?

Using electromagnetism

An electric motor uses electromagnetism to make its parts move. With large electric motors, the parts can be used to drive machinery. By following these instructions you could make your own model of a simple electric motor. On the next page you will find a picture of the motor, along with an explanation of how it works.

1. Pierce the matchbox and cork with the metal rod. Then wind a coil of insulated wire around the matchbox as shown. Wind tightly and neatly until you have covered the sides completely.

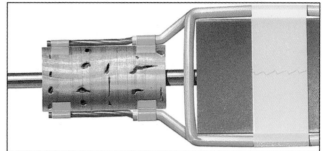

2. Draw the ends along the cork and strip 2cm (¾in) of insulation from each end. Then straighten the ends of the wire so they touch the cork, running along its sides. Tape the wires to the cork as shown in the picture above.

3. Build a mount for the motor using the wooden board. Make little holes for a split pin at each end of the board. Make sure that the pins are high enough to allow the motor to spin freely when it is mounted on them.

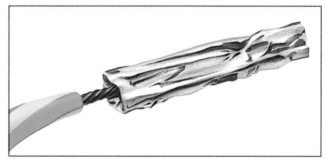

4. Fold the two 6cm (2½in) squares of kitchen foil until they can stand up firmly. Then take the two 25cm (10in) lengths of wire and strip 2cm (¾in) of insulation from the ends. Tuck one end of a wire into each brush.

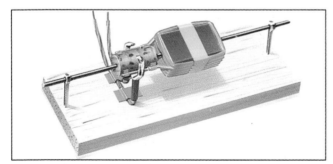

5. Bend the pieces of foil and tape them on the baseboard so they will brush evenly against the wires that are taped to the cork. Rest the motor on its supporting pins, and adjust the brushes so they will not stop it from rotating.

Mount the magnets on pieces of cork.

6. Place a magnet on either side of the motor. The north pole of one should point at the wires from one side, while the south pole of the other should point at the wires from the other side. Tape the free ends of the wires to a 9v battery.

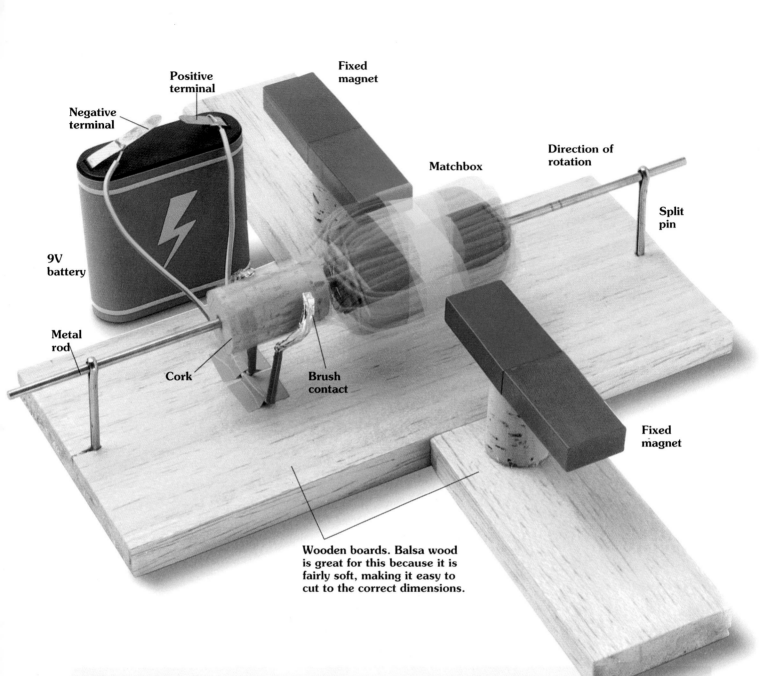

Positive terminal

Negative terminal

Fixed magnet

Matchbox

Direction of rotation

Split pin

9V battery

Metal rod

Cork

Brush contact

Fixed magnet

Wooden boards. Balsa wood is great for this because it is fairly soft, making it easy to cut to the correct dimensions.

What happens?

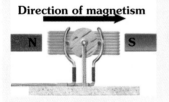

Direction of magnetism

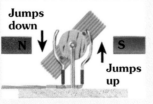

Jumps down

Jumps up

Flow of electricity breaks.

Flow of electricity begins again.

1. Before the wires are connected to the battery, there is only one magnetic force working – from north to south between the two magnets. (On a bar magnet, the red end is usually the north pole, while the blue end is the south pole.)

2. By connecting the battery to the wire, you make a second magnetic force – through the wire around the matchbox. The two forces affect one another, causing the wire on one side of the coil to jump up, while the wire on the other side jumps down.

3. As the wire jumps, it starts to rotate (because it is coiled around the matchbox, which pivots on the metal rod). As they move, the ends of the wire taped to the cork stop touching the brushes. This breaks the flow of electricity through the wire.

4. The coil should revolve until the wires touch the other brushes. Then the same forces start acting on the wires again. This makes them jump up again on one side and jump down on the other side. So the matchbox moves around... and around.

THE NATURAL WORLD

In this section there are lots of projects which will show you how to investigate the ever-changing natural world.

You can find out how to grow plants from dried seeds and you can do tests to see which conditions plants need in order to grow best.

You can also see how to set up your own weather station and build environments for creepy crawlies.

Weather watching

Weather can change dramatically from day to day. By following the instructions on these two pages you can create your own weather station to record your local weather. You may even be able to notice particular weather patterns and make your own forecasts.

Bottle thermometer

Thermometers measure the temperature of things around them. This one works because water in it expands as it heats up and contracts as it cools down. It is easy to make and works really well.

> ### You will need
> • Glass bottle • Food dye • Bowl • Water
> • Narrow drinking straw • Playdough
> • Cardboard strip 12 x 5cm (4¾ x 2in)
> • Ballpoint pen • Adhesive tape

Food dye

1. Fill the glass bottle with cold water. Add some drops of food dye to the water, then top up the bottle with water until it overflows.

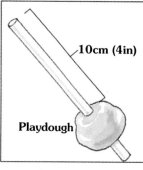

10cm (4in)

Playdough

2. Roll some playdough around the straw about 10cm (4in) from the top. Be careful not to crush the straw when you do this.

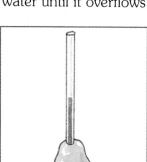

3. Put the straw in the bottle. Push the playdough around the top of the bottle, so the bottle is airtight. Water should rise up the straw.

4. Stand the bottle in cold water for a while. The water in the straw should fall. Now take the bottle outside and put it somewhere safe.

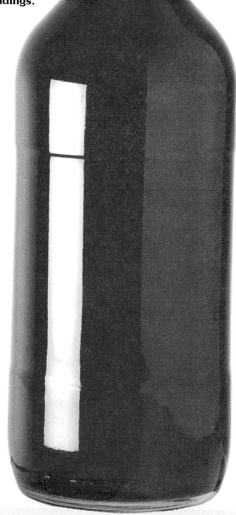

For a scale, mark the cardboard strip at 1cm (½in) intervals. Number the markings 1-10. Tape the scale to the straw.

Take readings at regular intervals, such as first thing in the morning, at lunchtime and in the evening. Try to keep a record of your readings.

Compare readings from different times of the day. Can you see any pattern to the temperatures?

What happens?

If the air temperature is warmer than the water in the bottle, the water expands. This forces the water up the straw. If the air is cooler than the water, the water contracts. This makes it shrink down the straw, giving a lower reading on the scale.

Wind speedometer

When the wind blows on the plastic sails of this simple instrument, it makes them spin around. By counting the number of spins in a certain time, you can record the wind's speed. Then you can see how it changes from day to day.

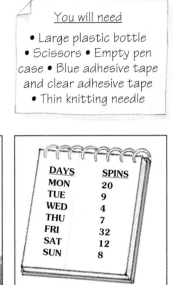

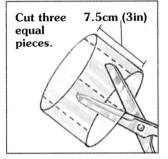

Cut three equal pieces. 7.5cm (3in)

1. Cut a 7.5cm (3in) section from the middle of the plastic bottle. Cut it into three parts and trim them to the same size.

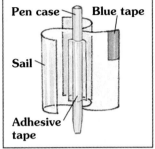

Pen case — Blue tape
Sail
Adhesive tape

2. Tape the plastic sails to the pen case. Stick blue tape to the top corner of one sail, so you can watch it as the sail spins.

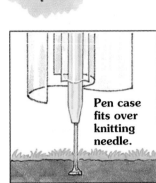

Pen case fits over knitting needle.

3. Push the blunt end of the knitting needle into the ground. Slip the pen case over the other end, so it rests on the needle's point.

DAYS	SPINS
MON	20
TUE	9
WED	4
THU	7
FRI	32
SAT	12
SUN	8

4. Each day, count how often the wind makes the sails spin in a fixed time, such as 30 seconds. Compare your results day by day.

Model barometer

Air always pushes against everything. This is called air pressure. Different weather conditions make the air pressure change. You can make something to measure air pressure, called a barometer.

1. Cut the neck off the balloon, then stretch it over the mouth of the jar. Fasten it tightly with the rubber band so the air cannot get out.

2. Cut off one end of the straw to make it pointed. Then stick the other end to the middle of the stretched balloon using adhesive tape.

3. Tape a piece of cardboard behind the jar so the pointer touches it. Make a mark at that point. Draw a scale above and below this mark.

What happens?

The barometer shows when the air pressure outside the jar becomes higher or lower. When it becomes higher, the air pushes hard on the balloon so the straw points up.

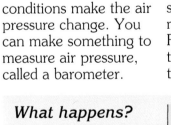

High pressure

When the air pressure is lower the air inside the jar pushes up on the balloon more than the air outside pushes down. This causes the straw to move so it points down.

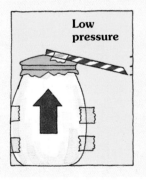

Low pressure

Plants' waterways

These experiments show how water travels through the stems of plants and into their leaves. They are fun to do and they have some amazing results.

Freaky flowers

<u>You will need</u>
- Jar • Blue food dye • Water
- White flowers such as carnations

1. Pour some water and several drops of blue food dye into the bottom of the jar. Then put the flowers in the jar.

2. After a day or so what starts to happen to the flowers? What happens if you leave them for three days?

What happens?

The dyed water is sucked up the flowers through the stems. At first, you see the dye at the tips of the flowers. After three days nearly all the flower will have been affected by the dye.

Short-stemmed flowers change faster than long-stemmed flowers because the water has less distance to travel to the petals.

You could arrange your flowers in a jar once you have finished the experiment. They should last for days.

The more blue dye you use in the water, the stronger the blue will be when it reaches the flowers' petals.

In this arrangement, the lighter flowers have been in dye for one day. The darker flowers have been in dye for three days.

Silly celery experiment

In some plants, such as celery, you can see the veins that carry water fairly clearly. Try this experiment to make them show up even more.

> **You will need**
> • Jar • Celery stem • Water
> • Red food dye • Knife

Fill the bottom of the jar with water and add a few drops of red food dye. Then put a celery stem in the water. Check the celery every hour or so. After a while can you see a change in the way it looks? If you leave it long enough, the celery will change even more. Are the leaves at the top of the stem affected too?

What happens?

The celery leaves need water to help them keep the celery alive. They pull the red-dyed water up through the veins in the stem of the plant. Because the veins are wide you can see them turn red as well as the leaves.

It's a fact!

The plant with the largest leaves is the Raffia Palm tree. Each leaf can reach more than 20m (54ft) in length.

Escaping water

When plants take in water, they don't always use all of it. Try this experiment to see what happens to the water that plants don't use.

> **You will need**
> • Potted plant • String
> • Large, clear plastic bag

Do not tie the string too tightly around the stem.

1. Cover the plant with the plastic bag and tie it around the stem. Stand it in a sunny place.

2. After four hours, rub the bag with your fingers. Can you see tiny water droplets?

What happens?

Plants do not use all the water that they take up. They get rid of extra water through tiny holes in their leaves. In this experiment, the bag traps the droplets that escape from the leaves, so you can see them.

INSTANT EXPERT

How do plants get water?

Most plants suck up water through their roots, which have tiny holes in them. The water travels to the leaves through the veins in the stem, which are called xylem vessels.

The water that is not needed escapes through holes in the leaves, called stomata, and evaporates. This helps pull more water up through the plant. The flow of water through the plant is called transpiration.

Water flow

Roots

It's a fact!

Some types of cactus, such as the Saguaro cactus, can expand their stems like fans so that they can hold as much water as possible when it rains.

Growing seeds

These experiments investigate seeds and show you how to help them grow into healthy plants. Growing your seeds will take a few weeks – it is fascinating to see how they sprout and develop day by day.

Looking at seeds

Plants make seeds so that new plants can grow. Seeds come in different shapes and sizes. They are often inside a fruit or a tough cover such as a shell or pod.

Beans are the seeds of bean plants.

A scar shows where the bean was attached to its plant.

Nuts are protected by a shell.

A tough case gives good protection.

Peas are encased in a protective pod.

Pits are the seeds of some fruit. Others have stones.

To look inside a dried bean, start by soaking it in water to make it soft. Then split it open carefully.

This is the young plant, ready to grow.

This is the young plant's food storage.

Sprouting seeds

You will need
- Dried kidney beans
- See-through jar • Water
- Kitchen paper towel

1. Line the jar's sides with a kitchen paper towel and add a little water. Put some dried kidney beans next to the glass, between the paper and the jar. Then stand the jar indoors, somewhere warm and dark, and wait for a week.

Paper towel

Beans

Water

2. The beans should germinate (sprout shoots and roots). They are now ready to grow into fully formed plants.

Shoot

Root

3. Leave the jar in a light place for about a week. Look at the seeds each day. How do they change?

What happens?

The plant grows and grows. Roots reach to the jar's bottom. At the top two small leaves, called seed leaves, grow first. Then bigger leaves sprout.

The seed cases wither away. They are not needed any more.

The shoots grow leaves.

More roots grow from the first one.

Plant growing experiment

You will need
- 3 sprouting seeds (see previous page)
- 3 plastic flower pots • Potting soil
- Pencil • 3 saucers or dishes • Pen

1. Fill the three pots with damp potting soil. Poke a hole in the soil with the pencil, deep enough for the roots. Put a dish under each pot.

2. Carefully take the paper towels with the growing seeds out of the jars (see previous experiment). Lift off the seeds and plant one in each pot. Push the soil down firmly around each seed.

3. Label the three pots. Put pot 1 near a window. Water it every three days. Put pot 2 near a window but do not water it. Put pot 3 in a dark cupboard and water it every three days.

4. Each day for three weeks, measure the plants to check how fast they are growing. Keep a record of their heights.

The roots will spread out in the pot and keep the plant steady.

What happens?

At first the plant in pot 3 will grow fastest. It grows fast because it is seeking the light. Because it needs light to grow, after a few days it grows more slowly. After three weeks, the plant in pot 1 should have grown best. It has soil, light and water. Plants need all these things to stay healthy.

If your plant grows very tall and starts to lean, tie it to a stick to keep it straight.

It's a fact!

If seeds remain dry, they will keep for years without growing. In the desert, seeds lie in the ground until there is enough water to make them grow. After rain lots of desert flowers appear.

INSTANT EXPERT

How do plants make food?

Plants make food by using a green substance in their leaves, called chlorophyll. This soaks up energy from sunlight.

Plants use this energy to turn carbon dioxide and water into a kind of sugar. They take in carbon dioxide from the air and water through their roots. Tubes in the stem carry the sugary food to all parts of the plant.

Sunlight

Carbon dioxide

Chlorophyll is in the leaves.

Food made here

Water is soaked up by the roots.

More things to grow

These projects involve growing plants not only from seeds, but also from flower bulbs, vegetable scraps and tree buds. The projects are easy to do but some take several weeks or even months so you will need to be patient to see your results.

Grow your own tree seedling

This experiment is best if you start it in the autumn. Start by collecting fresh, ripe seeds from trees in your area. It will take about two months for the seeds to sprout (some seeds may take longer).

You will need
- Flower pots • Stones • Saucers • Soil
- Plastic bags • String or rubber bands
- Seeds (for example acorns, chestnuts, sycamore seeds, apple or orange pits)

1. Soak your acorns (or other seeds) in warm water overnight. Peel off the hard outer shells with your fingers. Do not cut the shells from the nuts.

2. Put a handful of stones in the bottom of the flower pot. These will help the water to drain away properly. Place a saucer under the pot.

3. Fill the flower pot with some fresh soil or special potting soil until it is about two-thirds full. Now water the soil until it is moist, but not soggy.

4. Place one acorn on top of the soil. It will need a lot of room to grow so only put in one acorn.

5. Now cover the acorn with a layer of soil. This layer should be about as thick as the acorn itself.

Fasten with string or a rubber band.

The air in the bag keeps the soil moist.

6. Tie a plastic bag over the pot. This will keep the seed moist without watering. Put the pot in a sunny place and wait.

The soil should be moist but not wet.

7. As soon as the seedlings appear, remove the plastic bags. Water the seedlings once or twice a week.

8. When spring comes plant the little trees outside. Alternatively, put the pots outside and plant them in the ground next year.

Water the seedling often.

9. To plant a seedling, dig a hole a little larger than the pot. Lift the seedling and soil from the pot and plant it in the hole.

Growing without soil

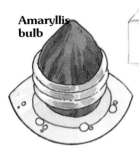

Amaryllis bulb

You will need
- Amaryllis bulb* • Water
- Jar with narrow neck

1. Fill a jar with water and place the bulb on top so that it touches the water. Leave the jar in a warm, dark place.

The green leaves will appear first.

2. After a few days the bulb grows roots and shoots. When this has happened, put the jar in the light. Does the plant grow successfully?

What happens?

The bulb doesn't need soil. It has everything inside it for a plant to start growing. The roots grow down to the bottom of the jar.

INSTANT EXPERT

What happens to plants in winter?

In winter some plants die right down to the ground. They store their food underground in a bulb. In the spring the plant starts to grow again using the stored food.

An onion is a bulb. Inside are lots of layers. These are the onion plant's food.

Sprouting carrot tops

Did you know you can grow plants from vegetable scraps such as carrot tops? A carrot stores food ready for a new plant to grow, just like a bulb.

You will need
- Carrot top • Saucer • Water

Don't let the water dry up.

Pour some water in the saucer and sit the carrot top in the middle. Leave it in a warm, bright place for two to three weeks. What happens to the plant?

What happens?

The carrot top begins to sprout leaves and gradually grows into a carrot plant.

After one week.

You could try growing other vegetable scraps too, from other uncooked vegetable tops.

After two weeks.

Opening winter buds

If left to themselves, many trees will only sprout leaves in the spring. Try this experiment in winter, to make twigs with buds on them sprout leaves.

You will need
- Scissors • Jar
- Twigs with buds on

Use scissors to cut some twigs. The best ones to try are horse chestnut, birch, willow and forsythia. Put the twigs in water and leave them in a warm, sunny spot indoors.

What happens?

The warmth makes it seem like spring. After a few days the buds will open.

* Amaryllis bulbs are available from gardening stores.

Animal watching

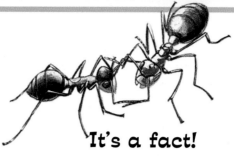

These projects help you find out more about the things small creatures eat and the ways they search for food. You will need to collect ants, woodlice and worms from grassy or soil-rich areas. Treat them carefully and make sure you put them back where you found them after you have finished studying them.

It's a fact!

Ants smell with little feelers on their heads, called antennae. When two ants meet they touch antennae. If they smell different it means that they are from different nests.

Where to find your subjects

Never pull on worms, or you may hurt them. They are covered with bristles that grip the soil tightly.

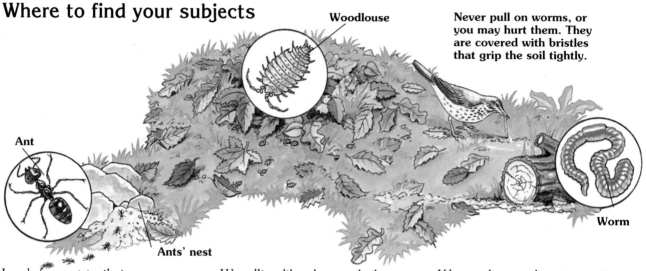

Woodlouse

Ant

Ants' nest

Worm

Look for ant trails in summer. At one end will be some food; at the other you should find the entrance to a nest.

Woodlice like damp, dark places. Look for them under logs, under piles of dead leaves and in walls.

Worms live under stones, in freshly dug soil or near compost heaps. They come to the surface at night.

Follow an ant trail

Ants live together in nests. When an ant finds some food it makes a trail for others to follow. To do this experiment, you will need to find an ants' nest.

You will need
• Sheet of paper • Small piece of apple
• Soil

1. Put the piece of apple on the sheet of paper and lay the paper close to an ants' nest. Wait for some ants to find the apple. They should all follow the same path.

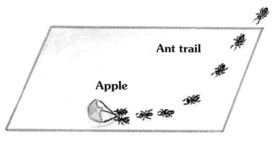

Ant trail

Apple

What happens?

Once an ant has found some food, it produces special chemicals that leave a scent trail. Other ants from the nest use their antennae, or feelers, to sense this scent. Even after the food has moved the ants still follow the old trail until a new one is laid.

2. Move the apple. Do the ants go straight to it? Now rub out the trail by sprinkling it with soil. The ants should scurry around for a while. Do they make a new trail?

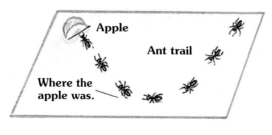

Apple

Ant trail

Where the apple was.

It's a fact!
The South American giant anteater can eat well over 30,000 ants a day.

Watching woodlice

Woodlice have sensitive antennae. Make this box, then collect six woodlice in a container. Watch how they find their way when you put them in the box.

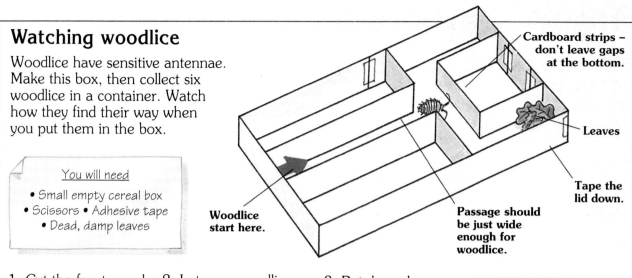

Cardboard strips – don't leave gaps at the bottom.

Leaves

Tape the lid down.

Passage should be just wide enough for woodlice.

Woodlice start here.

1. Cut the front panel off the cereal box. Then cut the front panel into three long strips. Use the strips to make the passages shown above.

2. Let your woodlice walk along the passage one at a time. When they reach the junction, some will turn left and some will turn right.

3. Put damp leaves in the right hand side of the box. Now let the woodlice walk through the box again. Which way do the woodlice go?

What happens?

The woodlice can sense the rotting leaves with their antennae. They use them to guide themselves to the food.

Make a wormery

To see how worms live and feed, make a wormery like the one shown here. Then find two or three worms to put in it.

It's a fact!

Worms are hard to study because they don't like the light. As soon as they sense it, they wriggle away, trying to find a dark place again.

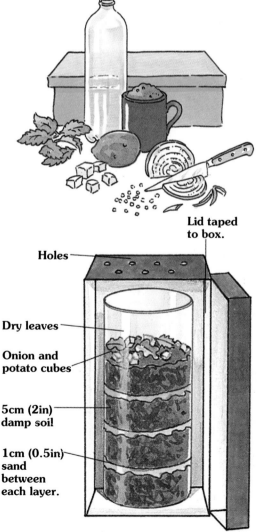

Lid taped to box.

Holes

Dry leaves

Onion and potato cubes

5cm (2in) damp soil!

1cm (0.5in) sand between each layer.

1. Tape one side of the shoe box lid to the box, so it opens like a door. Pierce holes in the top of the box with the pen to let air into the wormery.

2. Cut the top off the bottle. Then fill it with loosely packed layers of soil and sand, as shown here. Scatter potato and onion on the surface.

3. Gently drop in your worms and stand the wormery in its box with the door closed. Leave it outside in a cool, dry place for four days.

What happens?

After four days the layers of sand and soil will have been mixed together. The worms mix them by coming to the surface for food and then tunneling underground.

When you've finished this experiment don't forget to put the worms back where you found them.

Trapping the Sun's energy

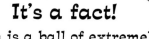

Energy from the Sun is called solar energy. Do these experiments on a warm sunny day to see how you can trap the Sun's heat to warm up water and cook food.

It's a fact!
The Sun is a ball of extremely hot gases. The temperature in its middle is 16 million°C (61 million°F).

Make a water heater

You will need
• Balloon • Long hose attached to water supply

A black hose is best for this experiment as it soaks up more of the Sun's heat.

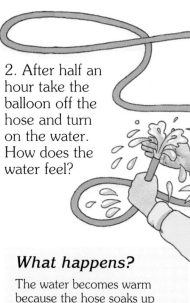

1. This experiment must be done outside. Coil a hose up so that as much of it as possible is in the sunlight. Attach it to the water supply and turn on the water. Turn it off when water comes out of the other end. Stretch a balloon over the end. Leave it for half an hour.

2. After half an hour take the balloon off the hose and turn on the water. How does the water feel?

What happens?
The water becomes warm because the hose soaks up the Sun's heat and warms the water inside.

Make a solar oven

This project shows you how to make a solar oven that is just about big enough to cook a few slices of apple or carrot. You will need to do this experiment on a warm summer's day, because you will need to use the warmth of the Sun.

You will need
• 2 disposable foam cups
• Large plastic pot such as a family-size yogurt pot
• Tissue paper • Baking foil
• Sheet of black paper
• Large sheet of stiff paper
• Plastic food wrap
• Some food (such as sliced carrot or apple) • Adhesive tape

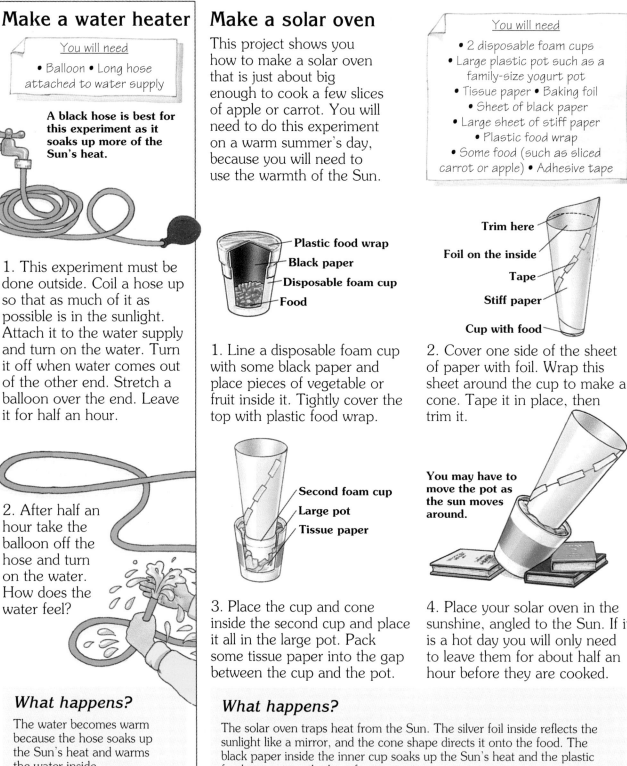

Plastic food wrap
Black paper
Disposable foam cup
Food

Trim here
Foil on the inside
Tape
Stiff paper
Cup with food

1. Line a disposable foam cup with some black paper and place pieces of vegetable or fruit inside it. Tightly cover the top with plastic food wrap.

2. Cover one side of the sheet of paper with foil. Wrap this sheet around the cup to make a cone. Tape it in place, then trim it.

Second foam cup
Large pot
Tissue paper

You may have to move the pot as the sun moves around.

3. Place the cup and cone inside the second cup and place it all in the large pot. Pack some tissue paper into the gap between the cup and the pot.

4. Place your solar oven in the sunshine, angled to the Sun. If it is a hot day you will only need to leave them for about half an hour before they are cooked.

What happens?
The solar oven traps heat from the Sun. The silver foil inside reflects the sunlight like a mirror, and the cone shape directs it onto the food. The black paper inside the inner cup soaks up the Sun's heat and the plastic food wrap stops the heat from escaping.

LIGHT AND DARK

How do mirrors work? Why are sunsets red? What is an eclipse of the Sun? You can find out in this section by doing tests that investigate all sorts of things to do with light and dark.

For example, you can find out how to make light bend around corners and how to split up light to make your own rainbow. You will also find instructions on how to make toys and gadgets that make use of light, such as kaleidoscopes and periscopes.

Bouncing light

When light meets a shiny surface such as a mirror it bounces off it and is reflected back. You can use reflections to create some strange and dramatic effects.

Bouncing spotlight

Try this test to see how light bounces off a mirror.

You will need
- Flashlight • Kitchen foil
- Rubber band • Mirror
- Ball • Pencil

Kitchen foil

1. Cover the end of the flashlight with kitchen foil and make a hole in the foil with the pencil. Put the flashlight on a table in a dark room.

2. Hold the mirror in front of the beam of light. Place the ball a short distance away and see if you can make the beam hit the ball. Try again with the ball in other positions.

You could try using baking foil or a metal lid from a jar instead of a mirror.

Light spot

What happens?

When light hits a surface at an angle, it is always reflected at an identical angle. To aim the beam in different places you need to change the angle of the mirror to the light, so the the light will bounce off at a different angle.

Beam of light   **Reflected light**

Shiny surface, such as a mirror.

Candle illusion

Here's a way to create a clever illusion using a sheet of rigid, clear plastic as a mirror and as a window at the same time.

1. Stand the plastic sheet between the two candles. Ask a friend to light one. Move the other one so your friend sees a reflected flame on its wick.

2. Now put your finger on the wick of the unlit candle. It will look as if your finger is burning.

3. Measure the distances between each candle and the sheet. You should discover that they are exactly the same.

You will need
- Sheet of rigid, clear plastic
- 2 small candles • Matches
- Playdough • Ruler

Rigid plastic sheet must be upright.

Use playdough to hold the frame in place.

What happens?

Your friend sees the unlit candle and your finger through the picture frame. At the same time, light from the lighted candle is reflected by the frame's shiny surface, so from where your friend is looking, your finger appears to be in the middle of the flame.

Reflected light from lighted candle.

Look from here to see both candles at once.

Light from unlit candle and finger.

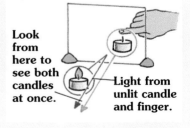

Kaleidoscope

A kaleidoscope uses mirrors to make ever-changing patterns. Follow the instructions below to make one out of mirror board. You could use little mirrors if you have them.

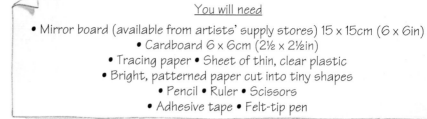

You will need
- Mirror board (available from artists' supply stores) 15 x 15cm (6 x 6in)
- Cardboard 6 x 6cm (2½ x 2½in)
- Tracing paper • Sheet of thin, clear plastic
- Bright, patterned paper cut into tiny shapes
- Pencil • Ruler • Scissors
- Adhesive tape • Felt-tip pen

The mirrors should face one another.

1. First cut some mirror board into three strips of equal width. Then tape the long sides of the mirrors together.

2. Stand the triangular tube you have made on some cardboard. Using the pen, draw around its shape and cut it out.

3. Tape the cut-out cardboard to the mirrors. When it is in place, push the pencil into the middle to make a hole.

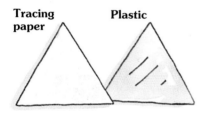

Tracing paper   **Plastic**

4. Place the triangular tube on the plastic sheet. Draw around the tube and cut out the shape. Repeat on some tracing paper.

5. Tape the plastic and tracing paper triangles together along two of their three sides. Put bright pieces of paper inside.

6. Tape the third side of the triangle. Then tape it to the open end of the tube, with the tracing paper on the outside.

7. What do you see when you point the end containing the paper bits to the light and look through the hole?

What happens?

The three mirrors reflect the shapes in a fancy pattern. The pattern will change when you shake the kaleidoscope.

It's a fact!

Moonlight is really light from the Sun that has bounced off the Moon's surface.

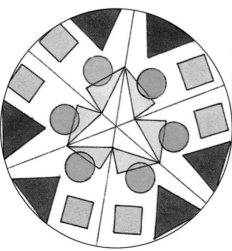

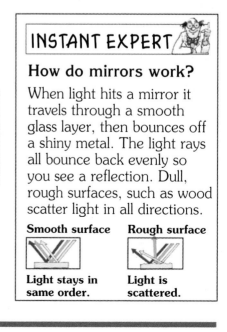

INSTANT EXPERT

How do mirrors work?

When light hits a mirror it travels through a smooth glass layer, then bounces off a shiny metal. The light rays all bounce back evenly so you see a reflection. Dull, rough surfaces, such as wood scatter light in all directions.

Smooth surface   **Rough surface**

Light stays in same order.   **Light is scattered.**

Splitting and mixing light

Light looks clear but it is really red, orange, yellow, green, blue, indigo and violet all mixed together. You can do simple tests to split and mix light.

Splitting light

You will need

• Flashlight • Black paper, to cover end of flashlight • Scissors • Clear plastic box • Mirror • Adhesive tape • Piece of thick white paper

1. Cut a small slit in the middle of the black paper and tape it over the end of the flashlight.

2. Fill the box halfway with water. Lean the mirror against the end of the box in the water.

3. Point your flashlight so the light beam shines on the mirror under the water. Then hold up some white paper so reflected light shines on it.

Narrow slit

Tape — Black paper

What happens?

Light travels in straight lines called rays. When light shines into water, the rays slow down and bend. The different shades all bend at slightly different angles. This makes the light separate into the shades of the rainbow. They are reflected off the mirror, out onto the paper, where you see them.

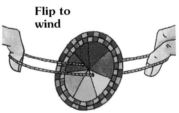

Red light bends least.

Light

Violet light bends most.

Mirror

Mixing disk

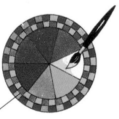

Paint squares around the edge, as shown here.

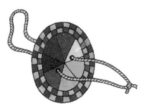

Flip to wind

1. Draw six lines from the middle of the circle to near the outer edge to make seven sections. Paint each section a different shade of the rainbow.

You will need

• Thick paper or cardboard • Red, orange, yellow, green, blue, deep blue and purple paint or felt-tip pens • Paintbrush • Pencil • String

2. Make two holes in the circle, about 1cm (½in) apart. Push the ends of some string, about 1m (3ft) long, through the holes. Tie the ends in a knot.

3. Hold the loops of string as shown. Flip the circle around to twist up the string. Then pull your hands apart to make the disk spin around.

What happens?

When the disk spins around at a very high speed your eyes see the different shades but they get mixed up in your brain. Because of this your brain sees a mixture of all seven shades, which is white.

INSTANT EXPERT

How do you see different shades?

When you see different shades, you are really seeing reflected light. Red things, for example, absorb all shades of light except red. They reflect red light back so you see them as red. White objects look white because they reflect back all the shades in the light. Black things absorb all shades of light.

Shades in an ordinary beam of light.

Red. Only red light is reflected. **Green.** Only green light is reflected **Black.** Nothing is reflected. **White.** Everything is reflected.

Seeing red

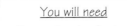

<u>You will need</u>
• Piece of red cellophane

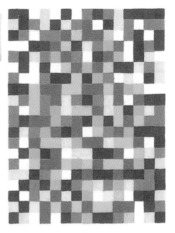

There is an object hidden among the shapes in this picture. Can you identify it?

Now hold a piece of red cellophane over your eyes and look at it again. Can you see it this time?

What happens?

The red cellophane stops all light except red from reaching your eyes. It makes all shades that don't reflect red, such as green and blue, look darker. However, all shades that reflect red look lighter.

Mixing shades

When you mix paints you get some very different results from when you mix different shades of light. Try mixing paints and then light to see what shades you make.

<u>You will need</u>
• Red, green, blue and yellow paint
• Paintbrush • White paper • 2 rubber bands
• Red, green, blue and yellow cellophane
• 2 flashlights of equal strength

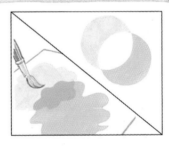

1. Use a paintbrush to mix equal amounts of red and green paint on white paper. What shade do you get?

2. Cover two flashlights with pieces of red and green cellophane, held in place by rubber bands.

3. Shine the flashlights onto a white surface. What shade do you see where the red and green light overlap?

4. Now mix blue and yellow paint and then blue and yellow light. Do you get the same results?

What happens to the light?

Red, green and blue are the main shades of light. Each time you add one to another you get closer to white. If you mix all three together they make white light. You can mix different strengths of red, green and blue light to make any shade.

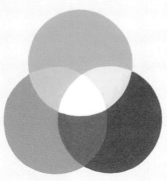

What happens to the paint?

Paints absorb all the shades of the rainbow except the ones that they reflect. For example, red paint reflects red light. Each time you add one shade of paint to another, you get closer to black, which does not reflect any light at all.

Playing with light

By playing around with the beam from a flashlight you can demonstrate some of the strange things that can happen to light. For instance, by shining the beam through glass or water you can get the light to bend or bounce.

Bouncing beam

This experiment is best performed in the dark. That way you can easily see where the flashlight's beam is sent when it passes through a container of water.

You will need
- Square glass or clear plastic container • Water
- 1 teaspoon of milk • Sheet of paper
- Thick book • Flashlight

1. Stand the square container, full of water, on the book. Prop up a sheet of paper at one side. Shine the flashlight directly at the container. The beam should come out on the other side.

2. Now shine the flashlight at an angle to the container of water. The beam does not come out of the water in a straight line, but at an angle, as in the picture above.

3. To see the beam clearly, stir the milk into the water. Then try shining the flashlight through the water from lots of different angles to see how the beam changes direction.

What happens?

When the beam of light enters the water, it goes in a straight line. The top of the water acts like a mirror and bounces the light back at the same angle.

Make light bend

You will need
- Flat bottle
- Water
- Milk
- Flashlight
- Small piece of cardboard

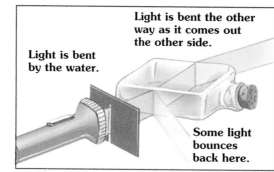

Light is bent by the water.

Light is bent the other way as it comes out the other side.

Some light bounces back here.

1. Fill a flat bottle with water and add a few drops of milk to it, so that the water turns cloudy.

2. Cut a narrow slit in the cardboard. In a dark room, place the cardboard in front of the flashlight so that you shine a thin beam of light at the bottle. In which direction does the beam shine?

What happens?

Light is always bent as it hits water and starts to travel through it. If it can pass through into air on the other side, it bends back the other way again – and carries on going in its original direction.

Magic coin

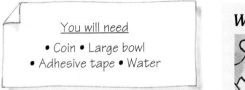

1. Tape the coin to the bottom of the bowl. Look over the edge of the bowl, then move back until you cannot see the coin any more.

2. Keep still and ask a friend to pour water into the bowl. What can you see now?

What happens?

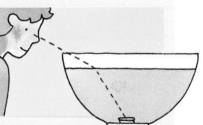

When the bowl is empty, the edge of the bowl stops you from seeing the coin.

When the bowl is full, the light bends so much that you are able to see the coin.

INSTANT EXPERT

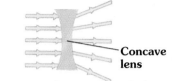

What is a lens?

A lens is a piece of glass or clear plastic that is shaped to make light rays bend.

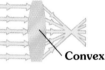

Concave lens

A concave lens makes light rays spread out. When you look through one, things look smaller.

Magnifying glasses are convex lenses.

Convex

A convex lens makes light rays bend inward. When you hold it close to things, it makes them look bigger.

Pouring light

1. Using the point of the scissors, carefully make a small hole in the plastic bottle. Hold your finger over the hole and fill the bottle with water. Then darken the room.

It's a fact!

Sometimes, on hot days, people think they see water far away. This is a mirage. It is caused by light from the sky being reflected off a layer of hot air near the ground.

If your flashlight has an adjustable beam, set it so that the beam is as narrow as possible.

2. Let the water pour out of the hole into a bowl and shine the flashlight through the bottle. Move the flashlight around. Does the stream of light sometimes get really bright?

For the best effect, pierce the bottle near the bottom.

The water in the bowl should light up.

What happens?

When the flashlight shines through the bottle at the correct angle, the stream of water should get very bright. It will probably be the brightest thing in the room, besides the flashlight.

This is because light from the flashlight gets bounced around inside the bending stream of water pouring out of the bottle. Scientists have a name for what is happening: total internal reflection.

When the stream of light looks duller, some of the light from the flashlight is bouncing out of the stream of water. This is because it is not shining in at the correct angle.

Daylight and dark

The Earth is constantly spinning and moving around the Sun. Because of this, some parts of the Earth's surface are lit and others are in shadow at different times. Try these experiments to find out more about sunlight, moonlight and shadows. You will need to do some of them in a darkened room.

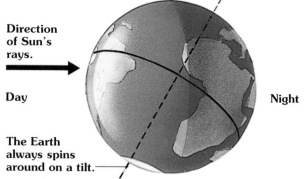

Direction of Sun's rays.

Day

Night

The Earth always spins around on a tilt.

Make a shadow clock

You will need
• Stiff cardboard • Sharp pencil
• Scissors

Shadows on the Earth keep moving as the Earth spins around. This shadow clock will help you find out about the way the Earth spins. You can use it to tell the time, but make sure that you put it in a place that will get plenty of sunshine.

1. Cut a circle from some stiff cardboard to make a dial. Push the pencil through the middle of it.

2. Push the pencil into the ground. Mark on the dial where the pencil's shadow falls each hour.

What happens?

The pencil's shadow moves steadily around the dial. This shows that the Earth spins at a steady speed. Shadows are long in the morning and late afternoon because the Sun is low in the sky. At noon, when the Sun is highest in the sky, they are very short.

Morning. Sun is low in the sky.

Noon. Sun is overhead.

Evening. Sun is low in the sky.

It's a fact!

The same side of the Moon always faces the Sun. The other side is always in darkness.

INSTANT EXPERT

How fast does Earth spin?

The Earth takes 24 hours to spin around once. It spins at over 1,600 kmph (over 1,000 mph).

Does the Moon spin?

No. However, it does revolve around the Earth – once every 28 days or so.

Does the Earth revolve?

The Earth revolves around the Sun. It takes a year for the Earth to complete one orbit.

The Earth moves around the Sun.

The Moon moves around the Earth.

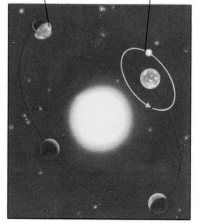

Make an eclipse of the Sun

Because the Earth moves around the Sun, and the Moon around the Earth, the Moon sometimes passes between the Sun and the Earth. This is called an eclipse of the Sun.

1. Stand the "Earth" and the "Moon" on a table with the Moon about 20cm (8in) away from the Earth.

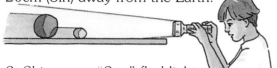

2. Shine your "Sun" flashlight directly at the Moon and Earth from about 60cm (2ft) away.

3. Look at the Earth. You should see a shadow that is dark in the middle and lighter on the outside.

What happens?

The Moon blocks out the Sun's rays and casts a double shadow on the surface of the Earth. The dark middle is called the umbra. The lighter outer shadow is called the penumbra.

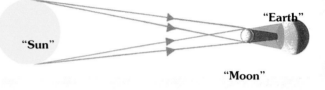

"Sun"　"Earth"　"Moon"

Make your own sunset

At sunrise and sunset, when the sun is low, the sky often looks red. During the day, when the Sun is overhead, the sky looks blue. Try this experiment to find out why the sky changes.

1. Fill the glass jar with cold water. Stir in one teaspoon of milk. In a darkened room, hold the flashlight to the side of the jar. The water should look blue.

2. Now move the flashlight around so it is shining through the jar at you. The light from the flashlight should look yellow, just like the Sun when it is shining.

3. Stir two teaspoons of milk into the water. Hold the flashlight to the side of the jar. The water should look blue. Now hold it so it shines at you. Does the water look pink?

What happens?

The milk makes the water go cloudy and this stops most of the light from passing through. Only the red parts of the light can get through the milky water.

A similar thing happens to the Earth at sunset. The Earth is wrapped in a blanket of air full of tiny pieces of dust and water too small to see. When the Sun is low in the sky, the light travels farthest to reach you and only the red parts can get through the dust and water.

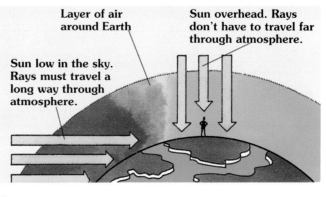

Layer of air around Earth

Sun overhead. Rays don't have to travel far through atmosphere.

Sun low in the sky. Rays must travel a long way through atmosphere.

73

Make a periscope

A periscope uses mirrors to let you see above walls or around corners. It is fairly easy to make, but you must put the mirrors in the right place for it to work.

You will need
• Cardboard 60 x 45cm (24 x 18in) • Scissors • Pencil
• Pen • Adhesive tape • Glue • Mirror board 24 x 10 cm
(9½ x 4in) or two mirrors 12 x 10cm (4¾ x 4in) • Ruler

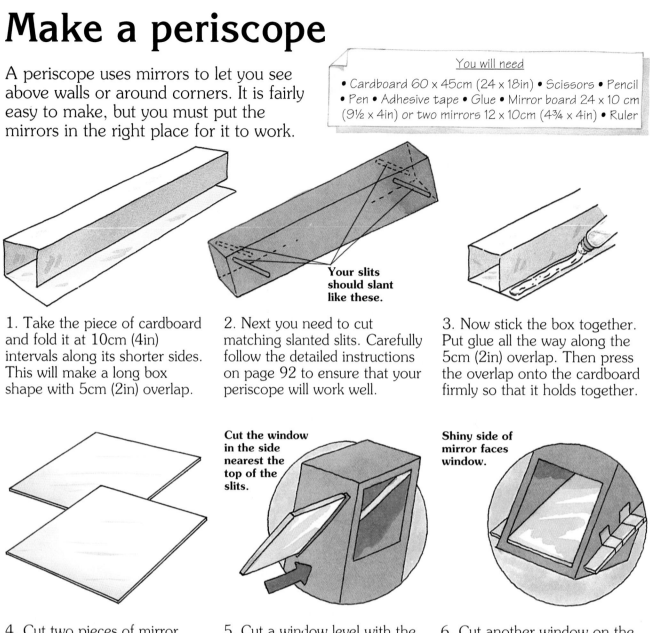

Your slits should slant like these.

1. Take the piece of cardboard and fold it at 10cm (4in) intervals along its shorter sides. This will make a long box shape with 5cm (2in) overlap.

2. Next you need to cut matching slanted slits. Carefully follow the detailed instructions on page 92 to ensure that your periscope will work well.

3. Now stick the box together. Put glue all the way along the 5cm (2in) overlap. Then press the overlap onto the cardboard firmly so that it holds together.

Cut the window in the side nearest the top of the slits.

Shiny side of mirror faces window.

4. Cut two pieces of mirror board (available from artists' supply stores) into rectangles 12 x 11cm (4¾ x 4¼in), or use mirrors that have these sizes.

5. Cut a window level with the top slits. Slide a mirror through the slits so the shiny side faces the window. Hold the mirror in place with strong adhesive tape.

6. Cut another window on the opposite side of the box, level with the other two slits. Slide a mirror through them. Secure the mirror with tape.

7. Point the periscope over a wall and look through the bottom window. You should be able to see what is on the other side.

What happens?

Light from the objects that you look at travels to the top mirror. It is bounced off the top mirror at an angle so that it travels down the thin cardboard box.

Then the light bounces off the bottom mirror and changes direction so that it is directed out of the box. If you are standing in front of the bottom mirror you should be able to see the reflection.

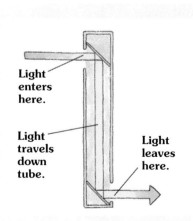

Light enters here.

Light travels down tube.

Light leaves here.

PUSHING AND PULLING

Did you know that with the force of your own breath you can make a ball defy gravity, or that you can turn a bucket of water upside down without spilling a drop?

All these experiments look at forces – what pushes on things, what pulls on them, what makes them move and what stops them from moving. You can also see how to make models that show the forces at work.

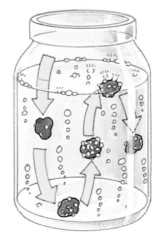

Falling to Earth

Things fall through the air because they are pulled down by a force called gravity. Try the experiments on these two pages to discover more about the force of gravity and how the weight and shape of something affects the way it falls.

<u>You will need</u>
(for the projects on this page)
• 5 pieces of paper, all the same size and weight
• Heavy stone

Falling race

Hold a piece of paper in one hand and a stone in the other. Which is heavier? Which do you think will fall faster?

Screw the piece of paper into as tight a ball as you can. Drop the stone and paper from the same height, at the same moment. Which lands first?

What happens?

The paper ball lands at the same time as the stone. This is because the effect of gravity is the same on both objects.

Paper race

1. Take two pieces of paper and crumple one into a ball as you did for the last test.

2. Drop them from the same height, at the same moment and watch when they land.

3. Try this a few times. Why do you think the flat paper always falls more slowly?

What happens?

As the two sheets of paper fall, air presses up under them. This stops them from falling so fast. The flat paper falls more slowly than the crumpled one because it has a larger area, so more air is trapped underneath it.

Lots of air.   Not much air.

Trick paper

Take two sheets of paper and write "heavy" on one and "light" on the other. Ask friends if they can think of a way to drop the papers from the same height at the same time and make the "heavy" one land first.*

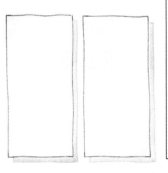

INSTANT EXPERT

What is gravity?

Gravity is a force that pulls objects toward each other. Every object has gravity but it is usually very weak. Gravity is only noticeable if one of the objects is truly massive, such as the Earth or another planet.

* To solve the puzzle they must crumple the piece of paper marked "heavy" into a ball.

Parachute tests

You will need
- Tissue paper
- Adhesive tape
- Thread
- Paper clips

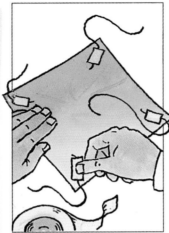

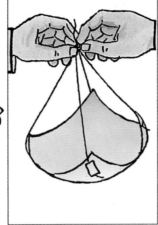

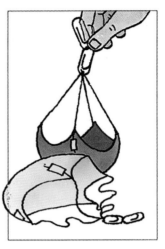

1. To make two parachutes of different sizes cut two squares of tissue paper, 30 x 30cm (12 x 12in) and 20 x 20cm (8 x 8in).

2. Using adhesive tape, attach threads about 15cm (6in) long to each corner of each of the pieces of paper.

3. Tie each set of four threads together. Make sure the taped ends of the threads are attached to the outside of the parachute.

4. Hook two paper clips onto each of the parachutes so they both have an equal amount of weight attached to them.

5. Stand on a chair or a table and drop the parachutes (be careful). Do they land at the same time? What happens if they have more paper clips on?

What happens?

Gravity pulls the parachute down, but as it falls, air is trapped under the canopy. The trapped air pushes up against the canopy, making the parachute fall slowly.

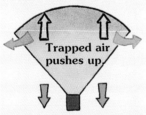

Trapped air pushes up

The large parachute should fall more slowly. However, its size can make it collapse, causing it to plummet to the ground. Adding paper clips should make it more stable, allowing it to fall slowly and smoothly.

You could make your parachutes in lots of sizes. See which floats best.

To make your parachute fall more smoothly, try cutting a small hole in the top of the canopy. This will let the air escape more evenly.

It's a fact!

Parachutes were invented in 1797. The inventor jumped from a hot air balloon and, wearing his parachute, floated safely to the ground.

Balancing tests

If you drop something, such as a ruler, gravity pulls it to the ground. If you rest its midpoint on your finger, gravity pulls equally on both sides and the ruler balances. Try these experiments to find out how to make things balance or fall over.

Make a mobile

Mobiles balance perfectly when gravity pulls equally on every part of them. Make the one below and experiment to find out how to make it balance.

> **You will need**
> • Thin garden cane 75cm (30in) • Sharp knife • Glue • Kitchen foil • Empty cereal box • Pencil • Needle • Strong thread • Adhesive tape

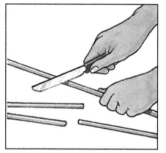

1. Using the sharp knife, cut the thin garden cane into one 30cm (12in) length and three 15cm (6in) lengths.

2. Cut the side off the cereal box, then glue the kitchen foil onto both sides of the cardboard, with the shiny side facing out.

3. Draw five equal-sized stars, one bigger star and a crescent moon on the foil-covered cardboard. Then cut out the shapes.

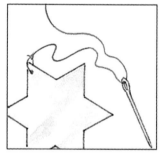

4. Use a needle to pull long pieces of thread through the tops of all the shapes. Then knot them securely close to the shapes.

Balancing the mobile

Knot or tape the stars on threads to the ends of the three short rods. Then balance each rod by hanging it from a loosely knotted thread and sliding the rod sideways until it hangs level. Secure the thread with a thin strip of adhesive tape or a knot.

Hang the three short rods from the long rod, as shown. One side of the long rod will point up. Tie the moon shape onto that side, then slide it sideways until the mobile is balanced.*

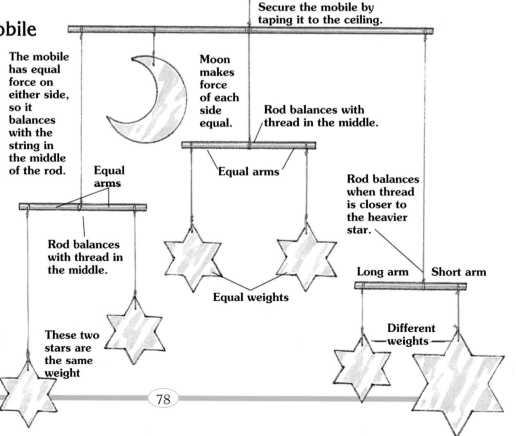

Secure the mobile by taping it to the ceiling.

The mobile has equal force on either side, so it balances with the string in the middle of the rod.

Moon makes force of each side equal.

Rod balances with thread in the middle.

Equal arms

Equal arms

Rod balances when thread is closer to the heavier star.

Long arm   Short arm

Rod balances with thread in the middle.

Equal weights

These two stars are the same weight

Different weights

(78)

* **If you have trouble balancing your mobile, see page 92.**

Perching parrot

This parrot balances and wobbles back and forth on the thin edge of a small piece of cardboard. You can see how it balances by making one for yourself. Start by tracing the template on page 93.

These markings are copied from a type of parrot called a macaw.

For the parrot to balance, the force pulling down has to be equal on both sides of this point.

1. Trace the parrot, cut it out and decorate it. Then make a slit in the middle of the small piece of cardboard and slot it onto the parrot's body. Stand the model on the edge of a shelf, table or even on your finger. Does it balance?

2. Add a bunch of about 25 paper clips to the bird's tail. Move the clips around, hanging the bunch to different parts of the tail. Where do the clips make the bird balance best?

3. Add a few more paper clips to the bunch. Is the bird's balance affected?

This bird is balancing on a simple stand. However, it works just as well perched on the edge of a shelf or a table.

What happens?

Without the paper clips the parrot will not balance. There is much more weight near the bird's head than its tail, so its head pulls down with more force than the tail.

To make the bird balance successfully, you need to make the force pulling down from the tail equal to the force pulling down from the head.

By adding more paper clips to the bunch you pull the tail with more force. To make the parrot balance again you have to put the clips in a different place.

Instead of paper clips, you could attach playdough to the tail to make the parrot balance.

Floating tests

Some things, such as stones, always sink. This is because stones are heavy for their size. The heaviness of an object compared to its size is called its density. Try the tests on these two pages to find out more about floating, sinking and density.

Sink the orange

> ### You will need
> • Orange • Bowl of water

Put a whole orange in a bowl of water. It should float. Now challenge a friend to make it sink. Probably, they will not be able to do it.

Peel the orange, then put it back into the water. What happens now? Does the orange float this time?

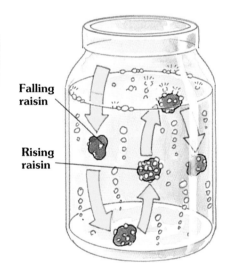

It's a fact!

Metal ships are very heavy but they are shaped so that they push aside a lot of water. The water pushes back hard enough to keep them afloat.

What happens?

The peeled orange sinks. Orange peel is full of trapped air bubbles. They make the orange light for its size, so the unpeeled orange floats. Without the peel, the orange is heavy for its size, so it sinks.

Raise the raisins

> ### You will need
> • A jar
> • Clear, carbonated drink
> • Raisins

Fill a jar (any size will do) with the carbonated drink and then drop in a handful of ordinary raisins. Watch for several minutes to see what happens. Do the raisins all stay still when they are in the liquid?

Falling raisin

Rising raisin

What happens?

First of all the raisins sink. Then gas bubbles stick to wrinkles on the raisins. The bubble-covered raisins then rise, because they are less dense than the drink.

At the top of the liquid the bubbles of gas burst. This makes the raisins denser than the drink, so they sink again.

INSTANT EXPERT
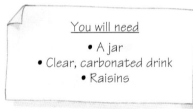

Why are some things denser than others?

In things that have a low density, such as cork, the molecules have lots of space in between each other. Things that have a high density, such as iron, have molecules that are packed together very tightly. If you put a piece of cork and a piece of iron the same size in water, the cork will float but the iron will sink.

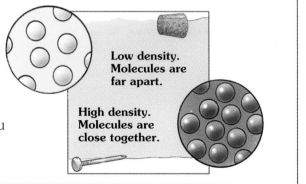

Low density. Molecules are far apart.

High density. Molecules are close together.

Float an egg

Normally, eggs sink when they are placed in water. This is because eggs are denser than water. Here is a way to make an egg float by making the water around it more dense.

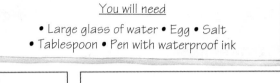

1. Gently lower the egg into the large glass of water. It will sink because it is more dense than the water. Remove the egg.

2. Add ten tablespoons of salt to the water and stir it until the salt has dissolved. The salt and water mixture is called brine.

3. Put the egg in the brine. This time it should float because the salt has made the water more dense than the egg.

Hold the egg in place as you mark it.

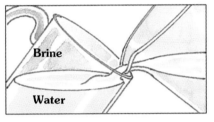

Brine

Water

4. Make a mark on the egg's highest point. Take out the egg and dry it. Draw a face, with the mark near the top.

5. Pour away half the brine so that the glass is half full. Tilt the glass gently, then slowly pour cold water on top of the brine.

6. When the glass is full, carefully slide in the egg. It should start sinking. Does it sink to the bottom?

What happens?

The water is less dense than the brine so it sits in a big layer on top of the brine.

The egg is denser than the water, but less dense than the brine. It sinks through the water but sits on top of the brine.

When you draw the face make sure you use waterproof ink, or the design will come off.

Tricks with air

Air pushes against you all the time, even though you cannot feel it. The tricks and experiments on these two pages show how air pushes and what happens when air moves at different speeds. Some of the results will surprise you.

Magic funnel

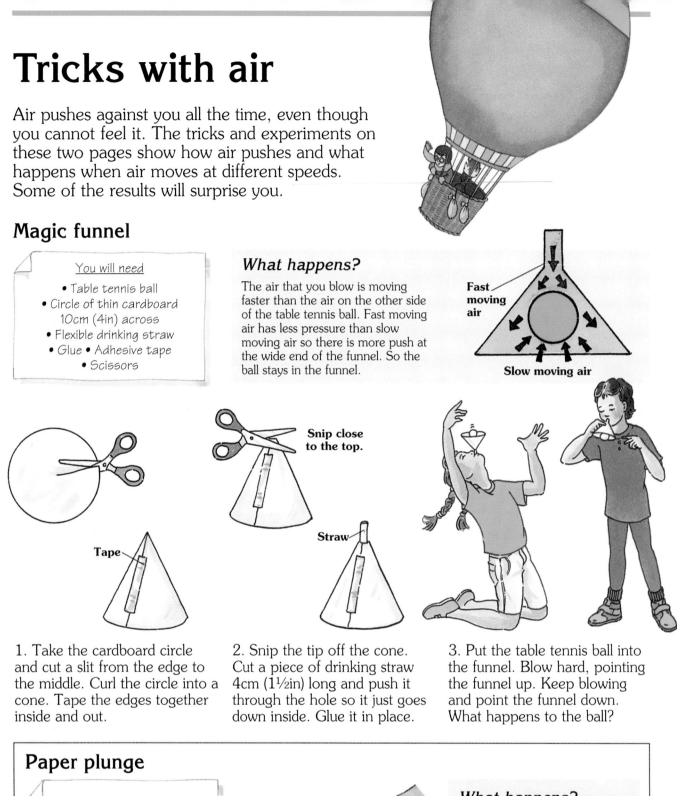

You will need
- Table tennis ball
- Circle of thin cardboard 10cm (4in) across
- Flexible drinking straw
- Glue • Adhesive tape
- Scissors

What happens?

The air that you blow is moving faster than the air on the other side of the table tennis ball. Fast moving air has less pressure than slow moving air so there is more push at the wide end of the funnel. So the ball stays in the funnel.

Fast moving air

Slow moving air

Snip close to the top.

Tape

Straw

1. Take the cardboard circle and cut a slit from the edge to the middle. Curl the circle into a cone. Tape the edges together inside and out.

2. Snip the tip off the cone. Cut a piece of drinking straw 4cm (1½in) long and push it through the hole so it just goes down inside. Glue it in place.

3. Put the table tennis ball into the funnel. Blow hard, pointing the funnel up. Keep blowing and point the funnel down. What happens to the ball?

Paper plunge

You will need
- Glass • Bowl of water
- Piece of paper

Crush the paper and push it firmly into the bottom of the glass. Plunge the glass straight down into the bowl of water. What happens to the paper? Where is the water level in the glass?

What happens?

Water can only get into the glass by squashing the air inside it. Air can be squashed (compressed) a little. However, it cannot compress enough to allow the water to reach the paper. It pushes back and stops the water from reaching the paper. Because of this the paper stays dry.

Sticking together

In this experiment, the air inside a container pushes out less strongly than the air outside pushes in. Try it to see what happens.

<u>You will need</u>

• 2 identical yogurt containers with flat rims
• Water • Small candle • Matches • Scissors
• Blotting paper 10 x 10cm (4 x 4in)

Tip the pot to light the candle.

Match rims exactly.

Be careful not to burn the pot.

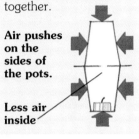

What happens?

As the candle burns it uses up the oxygen from the air inside the pots. This means there is less air in the pots pushing out. The air outside the pots pushes in and holds the pots together.

Air pushes on the sides of the pots.

Less air inside

1. Cut a 1.5cm (½in) hole in the middle of the blotting paper, then wet it thoroughly. Stand a small candle in a yogurt container and light the wick.

2. Cover the container with the blotting paper. Then stand a second yogurt container upside-down on top of the first, making sure the rims match exactly.

3. Wait until the flame goes out (20 seconds). Check that you have matched the rims exactly. If you have, what happens when you lift the top pot?

Empty the container

<u>You will need</u>

• Old plastic container with tight-fitting lid
• Ballpoint pen
• Adhesive tape
• Water

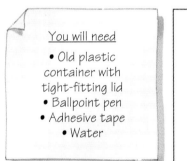

Hold gently.

This trick involves a leaky container of water. Can you stop the leak without covering the hole?

1. Make a hole in the base and lid of the container with a ballpoint pen. Tape over both the holes.

2. Fill the container with water and put on the lid. Gently pull the tape off the base. Does any water come out?

3. Pull the tape off the lid. What happens? Now try covering and uncovering the hole in the lid with your finger.

It's a fact!

You could not perform the experiments on these pages in outer space because there is no air and no gravity.

What happens?

When the hole in the lid is covered, the air below the container pushes up harder than the water in the pot pushes down. So the water doesn't pour out.

When you uncover the hole in the lid, the air above it pushes down on the water in the container. This helps it to push hard enough to flow out.

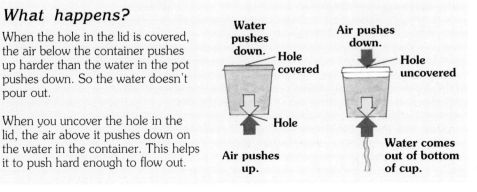

Water pushes down. **Hole covered**

Air pushes up. **Hole**

Air pushes down. **Hole uncovered**

Water comes out of bottom of cup.

Using pressure

The push, or pressure of moving air or water can be used to make things work and even to make electricity. Try the experiments on these two pages to find out more about water and air power.

Water jet test

> **You will need**
> • Empty plastic bottle
> • Pencil • Scissors • Adhesive tape

1. Take the top off the plastic bottle and make three holes in the side, one above the other. Use a pencil or the end of some scissors to do this.

2. Tape over the holes. Fill the bottle with water. Then quickly rip the tape off. Watch as jets of water spurt out. Which jet goes the farthest?

What happens?

The lowest jet of water should go farthest. Air presses down on the water at the top of the bottle. The water at the top presses down on the water beneath. This means that the water at the bottom is pushed out with the greatest force.

Make a water wheel

> **You will need**
> • 2 circles of cardboard 20cm (8in) across
> • 2 egg cartons • Waterproof paint or varnish
> • Paintbrush • Scissors • Stapler • 15cm (6in) nail
> • String • Pencil • Ruler • Wire

What happens?

The pressure of the running water pushes the water wheel around. The nail spins too. The pressure is great enough to lift the pencil attached to it. See if the wheel can lift other things.

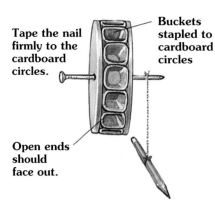

Tape the nail firmly to the cardboard circles.

Buckets stapled to cardboard circles

Open ends should face out.

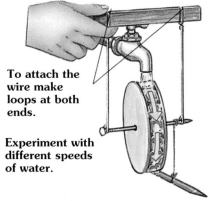

To attach the wire make loops at both ends.

Experiment with different speeds of water.

1. Make a small hole in the middle of the two cardboard circles. Cut up two egg cartons to make 12 small buckets. Paint or varnish them so that you make them waterproof.

2. Staple the buckets to the cardboard circles and place a nail through the holes. Tie the string tightly to one end of the nail. Attach the pencil to the other end.

3. Use some wire to hang the water wheel from a ruler or piece of wood. Now put it under running water. What does your water wheel do to your pencil?

Rocket balloon

Try this experiment to see how the pressure of the air inside the balloon can make it fly along like a rocket.

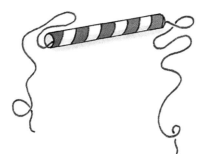

Tape loosely

The balloon should make a funny buzzing noise. This is the air rushing out as it empties.

1. Thread some string through a straw. Then tie it between two chairs, so that the string is held taut.

2. Blow up a long balloon and seal its neck with the clothes peg to stop the air from escaping. Tape the straw to the balloon.

3. Slide the balloon and straw back to the end of the string. Then take the peg off the balloon. Where do they go?

What happens?

When you take off the peg, the trapped air rushes out and makes the balloon move along. Scientists describe the way the balloon moves as "action and reaction". This means the movement in one direction (air rushing out backward) causes movement in the opposite direction (balloon moving forward).

It's a fact!

Rockets and jets work in the same way as the rocket balloon. Hot gases rush out from their rears and push them along.

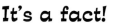

Simple windmill

Here's how to make a simple windmill. Windmills work in a similar way to water wheels, but use the power of the wind to make them spin.

What happens?

When you blow on the windmill, air gets pushed into the sails and makes them spin around.

1. Draw lines from corner to corner of the paper square. Then cut from near the corners to the middle.

2. Mark each corner, as shown. Bend the marked points to the middle and push a pin through them at the middle.

3. Slip a bead onto the pin, then push the pin into a stick. What happens when you blow the windmill?

It's a fact!

Huge windmills called wind turbines are used to make electricity. Some wind farms have hundreds of wind turbines. Wind farms need to be built in open areas where there is plenty of wind.

Flight tests

Have you ever wondered how planes fly? Make the models on these two pages and experiment with them to find out how a plane takes off, what keeps it up in the air and how its movements are controlled.

Make a model wing

The shape of a plane's wing helps it to stay in the air. Try this to find out how.

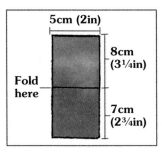

5cm (2in)

8cm (3¼in)

Fold here

7cm (2¾in)

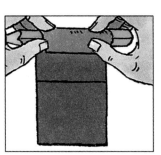

Tape here.

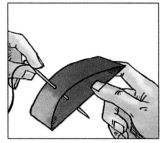

1. Fold the long side of the stiff paper 8cm (3¼in) from the end. Then unfold it.

2. Roll the longer end of the paper evenly around the pencil or pen to make it bulge.

3. Tape the ends of the paper together so the top is curved and the bottom is flat.

4. Push the thread through the wing, about a third of the way back from the fold.

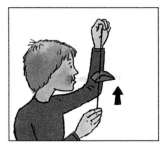

5. Hold the thread tight between both hands and blow at the folded edge of the wing. What happens?

What happens?

The wing should move up the thread. This happens because the air flowing over the curved top of the wing travels farther and goes faster than the air below, so it pushes down less on the wing.

The higher pressure air below pushes the wing up. This is called lift. It is the main force that keeps a plane in the air.

Faster air

Slower air

Lower pressure

Higher pressure

INSTANT EXPERT

How does a plane take off?

Power from the engine drives the plane forward. As it moves, air flows around the wings and creates lift. The lift increases as the plane moves faster. When there is enough lift to overcome gravity, the plane takes off. All the time, the plane is being slowed down by having to push through the air. This is called drag, and the engines have to overcome it.

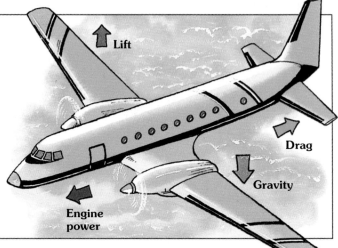

Lift

Drag

Gravity

Engine power

Make a glider

A glider has wings and a tail like a plane. It has two sets of flaps on the wings and tail to make it move in different directions.

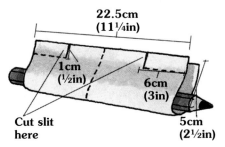

22.5cm (11¼in)

1cm (½in)

6cm (3in)

Cut slit here

5cm (2½in)

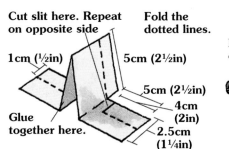

Cut slit here. Repeat on opposite side

Fold the dotted lines.

1cm (½in)

5cm (2½in)

5cm (2½in)

4cm (2in)

2.5cm (1¼in)

Glue together here.

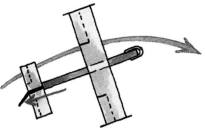

Paper clips

Tape

1. Fold the larger piece of paper lengthwise 6cm (3in) from one edge and roll the longer part around a pencil. Tape the long edges together. Cut two 1cm (½in) slits in the edge as shown.

2. Cut and fold the second piece of paper as shown in the picture above. The middle section should extend 1cm (½in) beyond the side sections to make a rudder.

3. Tape the wings and tail to a straw. Attach the paper clip to the front of the straw and test your glider. Attach more paper clips until the glider flies smoothly.

Controlling your glider's flight

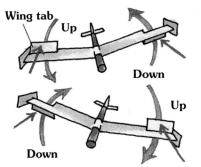

Wing tab

Up

Down

Down

Up

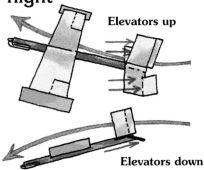

Elevators up

Elevators down

The wings give stability across the glider. You can disturb the balance as much as you need by moving the tabs on the wing edges up and down.

The tabs on the tail are called elevators. They control whether the glider climbs or dives when it flies. Adjust them to see what effect this has.

Here, the rudder is turned to the right, making the plane turn to the right.

By adjusting the rudder, plus the wing tabs and the elevators, you will be able to make your glider turn either to the right or to the left.

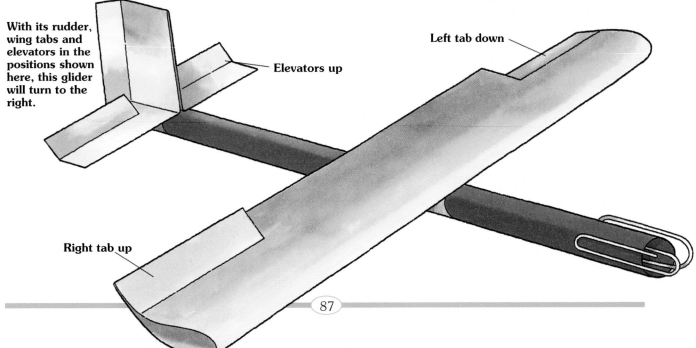

With its rudder, wing tabs and elevators in the positions shown here, this glider will turn to the right.

Elevators up

Left tab down

Right tab up

Turning and spinning

Moving objects always travel in straight lines unless something forces them to change direction. Forcing something to turn or spin quickly can have some unexpected results. Try the experiments on these two pages to see some of these effects for yourself.

It's a fact!

Fairground rides use the outward force of spinning objects to do things that look impossible.

Swing the bucket

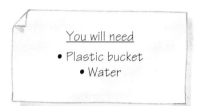

You will need
- Plastic bucket
- Water

Fill the bucket up to halfway with water. Stand outside and swing it in a circle above your head, as fast as you can. Does the water fall out of the bucket?

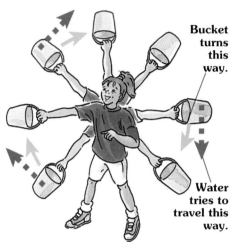

Bucket turns this way.

Water tries to travel this way.

What happens?

When you swing the bucket, you keep forcing it to change direction, but the water inside still tries to travel in straight lines. The water is pushed against the inside of the bucket and cannot fall out.

Beware. If you do not swing the bucket fast enough you will get a soaking.

Lift the pot

Is it possible for a pencil eraser to lift a pot of stones? Try this experiment to find out.

1. Make two holes on opposite sides at the top of the yogurt container with the pen. Thread string through the holes to make a handle. Tie a 40cm (16in) string to the handle and thread it through the pen casing.

2. Using the knife, carefully poke a hole through a pencil eraser (you might like to ask a grown-up to do this). Feed the string through the holes and tie it firmly.

3. Fill the yogurt container with stones and stand it on a table. Hold the pen casing and start to whirl the eraser around, as if you were swinging a lasso. What happens to the stones?

You will need
- Empty pen casing • Ballpoint pen
- Sharp knife • Pencil eraser
- Yogurt container • String
- Small stones

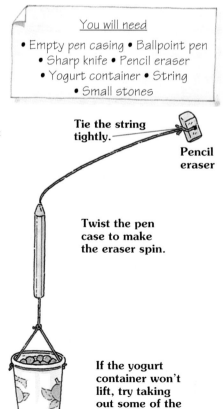

Tie the string tightly.

Pencil eraser

Twist the pen case to make the eraser spin.

If the yogurt container won't lift, try taking out some of the stones.

What happens?

The spinning eraser is flung away from the end of the pen casing, but the weight of the stones holds it back. Because of this, it moves in a circle. The more you whirl the pen casing, the faster the eraser spins. If you twist the pen casing enough, the pull of the eraser becomes stronger than the downward pull of the stones, and it lifts the pot.

As it spins, the eraser is always pulling out and trying to break free from the string.

The outward pull of the eraser is stronger than the downward pull of the stones.

Make a spin dryer

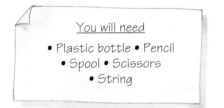
A spin dryer spins things around in a drum and the water is pushed out through holes in the sides. Follow the instructions here to make your own mini spin dryer. This experiment will make a mess, so it's best to do it outside.

Cut around here.

1. Push one blade of a pair of scissors into a plastic bottle, near the top as shown. Carefully snip all the way around to cut the top off neatly.

Make two holes near the top.

Make holes around the sides.

2. Poke holes in the bottom half of the bottle. Tie a piece of string through two holes at the top to make a handle. Tie a length of string to the handle.

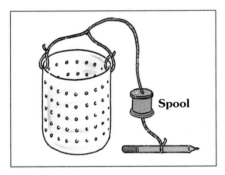

Spool

3. Slide an empty spool onto the length of string and then tie a long pencil to the end of the string, as shown above.

Wet cloth

4. Push pieces of wet cloth or wet paper towel into the dryer and press them down gently. Don't pack them in too tightly.

The faster you can turn the pencil, the more water will come out of the dryer.

5. Hold the spool in one hand and then wind the pencil around as fast as you can using your other hand.

What happens?

When an object spins, anything on its surface is flung off. This is caused by something called centrifugal force. When you make your dryer spin, water from the cloth is flung through the holes in the sides.

Washing machines use centrifugal force to get excess water out of clothes. The clothes are held in a metal cylinder (called the drum) that has holes in it. After the clothes have been washed, the drum spins around very fast. The clothes are pressed against the side of the drum and the water is flung out, leaving the clothes damp rather than soaking wet.

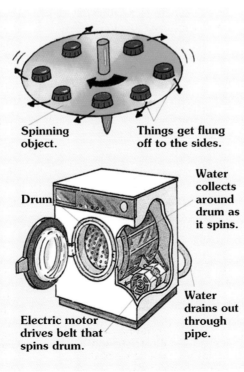

Spinning object.

Things get flung off to the sides.

Drum

Water collects around drum as it spins.

Electric motor drives belt that spins drum.

Water drains out through pipe.

It's a fact!

Satellites stay in orbit because the outward force as they spin is just balanced by the pull of the Earth's gravity. If they slow down, they fall down to Earth.

Starting and stopping

It can be hard getting an object to start moving, and even harder making it stop. Things try to stay still if they are not moving – or keep moving if they are already moving – because of something called inertia. The experiments on this page investigate inertia. Try the ones opposite to find out how to slow objects down.

Orange drop trick

> ### You will need
> • Orange • Postcard
> • Matchbox cover • Mug

To set up this trick, lay the postcard on the rim of the mug. Then stand the matchbox cover in the middle of the card and carefully balance an orange on top of it. When everything is in place, pull the card away very sharply. What happens to the orange?

What happens?

Heavy things, like the orange, have more inertia than light things, like the postcard and matchbox cover. Inertia stops the orange from getting moving, so it drops into the mug.

Pull sharply in this direction.

It's a fact!

When a car brakes hard or crashes, if the people inside are not wearing seatbelts, their inertia will keep them moving forward and they could go through the windshield.

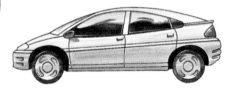

Coin challenge

> ### You will need
> • Five identical coins • Knife

1. Start by putting the five coins in a neat pile. Then challenge a friend to remove the bottom coin without touching the rest of the pile.

2. Knock the bottom coin sharply with the blunt edge of the knife. What happens to the coin that you hit? What happens to the other coins?

What happens?

The pile of coins is heavy so it has a lot of inertia and stays still when you knock the bottom coin. The bottom coin on its own is light, so it has less inertia and moves easily when you hit it.

Entertainers like to perform this trick using breakable things.

Stop the egg

Set a raw egg spinning on a plate. Then lightly touch it with your finger to stop it. As soon as the egg stops, take your finger away. What happens to the egg?

You will need
• Raw egg • Plate

What happens?

When you put your finger on the egg, you stop the shell but inertia keeps the white and yolk spinning. When you let go, the moving contents make the egg start spinning again.

A hard-boiled egg wouldn't start spinning again because its contents are solid.

Why does spinning make you dizzy?

If you spin around then stop suddenly, you feel dizzy. This is because of inertia. When you spin, liquid inside three tiny tubes within your ears spins too. When you stop suddenly, the liquid keeps on moving. Your brain thinks your body is still spinning, so you feel dizzy.

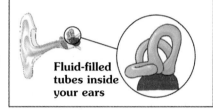

Fluid-filled tubes inside your ears

How brakes work

When two surfaces move over each other they rub together. This is called friction. Smooth surfaces slide over each other and create less friction. Try this experiment to show how you can use friction to slow down moving things.

You will need
• Matchbox • Matchstick
• Needle • Thread

1. Cut the matchstick to fit exactly across the matchbox tray. Wedge it in as shown.

You could decorate the matchbox as a spider.

3. Replace the matchbox cover. Hold the thread tight, then slacken it.

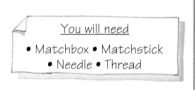

2. Using the needle, pass the thread through the matchbox and over the matchstick.

What happens?

When the yarn is tight, its surface presses against the matchstick. The surfaces rub together, which acts as a brake.

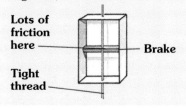

Lots of friction here

Brake

Tight thread

Adding oil

Surfaces have less friction if they are covered with oil. Try this test to prove it.

You will need
• Plastic tray • Cooking oil
• Bottle top

1. Using your finger and thumb, flick the bottle top so it skims across the tray. How soon does friction make it stop?

2. Cover the tray with a thin film of oil. Then skim the bottle top across it again. How far does it travel now?

What happens?

Oil lubricates the surfaces (stops them from rubbing against each other) – so the bottle top is not slowed down so quickly.

Tips and techniques

Detailed instructions for periscope (see page 74)

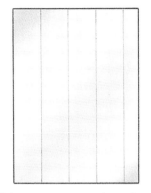

1. Take your piece of cardboard, which you should already have folded four times along its shorter sides. Lay it out flat, with the overlapping tab running down the right hand side of the piece.

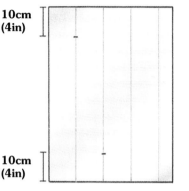

2. On the crease closest to the left of the cardboard, make a mark 10cm (4in) from the top. On the crease second closest to the left, make a mark 10cm (4in) from the bottom of the cardboard.

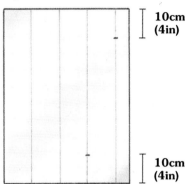

3. On the crease closest to the right of the cardboard, make a mark 10cm (4in) from the top. On the crease second closest to the right, make a mark 10cm (4in) from the bottom of the cardboard.

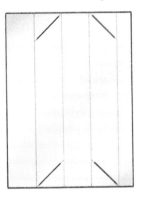

4. Using a pencil, lightly draw a straight line across from the marks you made in steps 2 and 3 to the nearest corner. Then, using a pen, draw over the pencil line, stopping 1cm (½in) from either end of the pencil line.

5. Put a ruler along the slanting lines and then draw a craft knife along the part marked with the pen. Press down firmly to make clean, accurate cuts. Be careful when you do this – craft knives can cut your fingers easily!

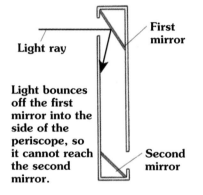

Make sure that you cut the slanting lines accurately, so that the mirrors line up when you put them in the periscope. If they don't line up the images will bounce off the mirrors in such a way that they do not reach your eyes.

Balancing a mobile (from page 78)

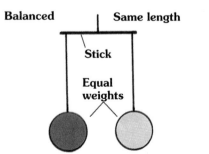

If both arms (the stick across the top that hangs out on either side of the thread from which it is suspended) are the same length, they balance equal weights.

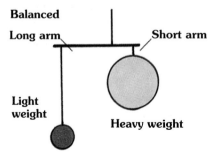

When the parts of a mobile do not balance, move the middle thread very gradually to the end that is pointing down. Eventually, the weights will become balanced.

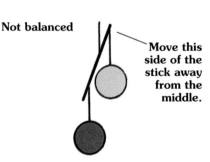

When you make a mobile you will need to balance each hanging piece one by one. Before you do this, you will need to hang all the pieces from their threads.

Tracing a template

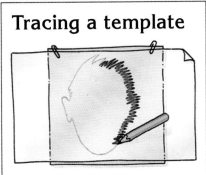

1. Lay some tracing paper over the template. Using paper clips, attach the tracing paper to the template. Trace the outline with a pencil.

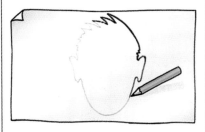

2. Unclip the tracing and turn it over. Draw over the outline in pencil, making sure that it is covered thickly. Turn the tracing over again.

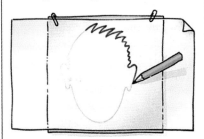

3. Lay the tracing on some cardboard or paper. Pressing fairly hard, go over the lines again, so that a line appears on the surface beneath.

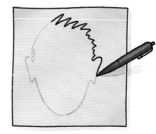

4. Remove the tracing paper. You should be able to see the tracing that has transferred onto the new surface. To make it more visible, go over the lines with a pencil or a ball-point pen.

Tracing the parrot (from page 79)

Trace all the lines on this template onto a piece of cardboard. Then cut out the outline shape, shown in red.

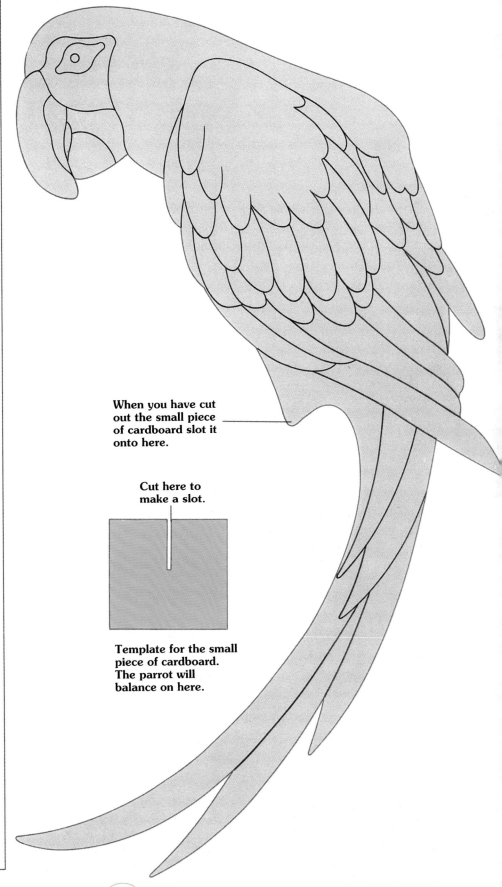

When you have cut out the small piece of cardboard slot it onto here.

Cut here to make a slot.

Template for the small piece of cardboard. The parrot will balance on here.

Glossary

Absorb   To suck up or take in.

Acid   Something that will react with a **base** to make a **salt**. A test for an acid is to dip **litmus paper** into it. Acids turn litmus paper red.

Air pressure   The **force** with which the air presses down on things. Air pressure changes all the time, depending on the weather. Also, it gets weaker as you get higher and higher above sea level.

Alkali   A **base** that can be dissolved in water. A test for an alkali is to dip **litmus paper** into it. The alkali will turn the litmus paper blue.

Antennae   The feelers on the head of an insect such as an ant.

Arteries   The **blood vessels** that carry blood from your **heart** to the rest of your body. (See also **Veins**.)

Atom   The smallest part of an **element** that still has the chemical properties of that element. Everything in the universe is made up of combinations of different atoms.

Baking soda   A white powder that is often used in cooking, in mouth washes and in some types of fire extinguishers. Its scientific name is sodium hydrogen carbonate.

Balanced   When things are of equal weight on either side, so that they do not tip or fall over.

Barometer   An instrument that measures **air pressure**.

Base   A substance that is the chemical opposite of an **acid**. When mixed with an acid it creates a **salt**. A base that can **dissolve** in water is called an **alkali**.

Biology   The scientific study of living things.

Blind spot   A small area inside your eye that is not sensitive to any light. It is the point where your **optic nerve** is attached to your eyeball.

Blood vessels   The tubes in your body through which your blood flows. (See also **Arteries**, **Veins**.)

Bulb   A short underground stem from which a new plant shoot grows.

Carbon   An **element** found in coal and all plants and animals. Diamonds are entirely made up of carbon.

Carbonate   A **compound** that contains a **metal** plus **carbon** and **oxygen**.

Carbon dioxide   A **gas** that is breathed out by people and animals. In large amounts, it will put out flames. It is also used to make soft drinks.

Centrifugal force   A **force** that tries to pull something away from the middle of something that is moving in a circle.

Chemistry   The scientific study of substances and the ways in which they react with each other.

Chlorophyll   The green substance in plants that allows them to use the Sun's energy to make food.

Chromatography   The process of separating parts of a **mixture** by letting it travel through a material that **absorbs** each part at a different rate.

Citric acid   A sharp tasting **acid** obtained from citrus fruit, such as orange, lemon, lime or grapefruit.

Coagulation   When a liquid becomes a soft, almost solid mass.

Compound   A substance made up of two or more **elements** that are chemically bonded together.

Concave lens   A **lens** with faces that are curved in, like the inside of a dish.

Conductor   A substance through which **electricity**, sound or heat can flow.

Contract   To become smaller.

Convex lens   A **lens** with faces that are curved out, like the outside of a ball.

Density   How heavy or light an object is for its size.

Dissolve   To break up into very small parts, especially when mixed with a **liquid**.

Domain   A piece of magnetic metal whose **atoms** are all pointing the same way. This means that the metal will act as a **magnet**.

Drag   The **force** that tries to slow down objects moving through **gases** or **liquids**.

Eclipse   To cut off the light between one thing and another, especially between planets and moons. (See also **Eclipse of the Moon**, **Eclipse of the Sun**.)

Eclipse of the Moon   When the Earth comes between the Sun and the Moon, so that all or part of the light to the Moon is blocked out.

Eclipse of the Sun   When the Moon comes between the Sun and the Earth, so that all or part of the Sun's light is blocked out.

Electrical charge   What results when an atom contains fewer or more **electrons** than usual. More electrons than usual gives a negative charge. Fewer electrons than usual gives a positive charge.

Electrical circuit   A complete path that an **electric current** can flow around.

Electrical switch   A device to open, close or divert the flow of an **electric current**.

Electric current   The rate of flow of an **electrical charge** from one place to another.

Electricity   A form of energy that is caused by **electrons** moving from one **atom** to another.

Electric motor   A machine that changes electrical energy into mechanical energy to produce movement.

Electromagnet   A **magnet** that can be switched on and off by **electricity**.

Electrons   One of the tiny parts of an **atom**, which carries a negative **electrical charge**.

Element   A substance made up of one kind of **atom**. It cannot be broken down to form simpler substances.

Enzyme   A chemical in the bodies of humans and animals, and in plants, which speeds up chemical reactions without being changed itself. Some enzymes can be made artificially.

Evaporate   To change from a liquid into a **vapor**.

Expand   To become larger.

Force   A thing that alters the shape or the movement of an object.

Freezing point   The temperature at which a **liquid** freezes or becomes **solid**. Water freezes at 0°C (32°F).

Friction   The **force** that tries to slow down touching objects that are moving over each other.

Gas   An air-like substance that will spread to fill the space that contains it.

Germination   The stage when a **seed** begins to grow to become a plant.

Gluten   A sticky mixture of **proteins** found in wheat and other grains. Makes dough tough and stretchy.

Gravity The **force** that pulls things toward each other. Gravity keeps you on the surface of the Earth and stops you from floating away.

Ice Water when it is frozen.

Indicator A substance for testing the strength of an **acid** or **alkali**. It changes color depending on the strength of the acid or alkali it is testing.

Inertia The tendency of a thing to resist a change in its movement. Inertia makes it hard to move something when it is still and hard to stop something when it is moving.

Insulator A substance that cannot conduct **electricity**, heat or sound very well. (See also **Conductor**)

Iodine A chemical element that is often used to make dyes to be used in photography or medicine.

Lens A substance that is transparent, which brings together or spreads beams of light that pass through it.

Lift The upward **force** created by an aircraft's wings as it moves through air.

Light rays The thin beams that come from a source of light.

Liquid A wet substance that can be poured.

Litmus paper Paper containing an **indicator** that turns red when touched by an **acid**, and blue when touched by an **alkali**. Made from plant-like organisms called lichens.

Magnet A material, usually made of **metal**, that can pull iron toward it.

Magnetic field The area around a **magnet** inside which iron will be pulled toward it.

Melting point The temperature at which a **solid** changes into a **liquid**. For example, ice melts at 0°C (32°F) to become water.

Metal A chemical substance, such as iron, copper, or silver, which is usually hard and shiny, is a good **conductor** of heat and **electricity**, and can be melted and formed into shapes.

Microbes Germs or other living things that are too small to be seen without a microscope.

Mirage Something that you think you see in the distance, such as water, which is not really there.

Mixture Two or more substances that are mixed together, but are not chemically bonded together.

Molecules Two or more **atoms** that are chemically joined together to form a particle that can exist on its own.

Nerves Thin fibers that send messages between your brain and other parts of your body, so that you can feel things and move.

Nitrogen An invisible **gas** that makes up about four-fifths of the Earth's air. It is an **element**.

Optical illusion Something that your brain thinks it has seen, but in fact does not exist. A **mirage** is an optical illusion.

Optic nerve A **nerve** that connects the eye with the brain, carrying images to the brain.

Oxygen An invisible **gas** found in the air, that humans and animals need in order to breathe, and flames must have in order to burn. It is an **element**.

Penumbra The dim outer edges of a **shadow** where some light gets through. (See also **Umbra**.)

Physics The scientific study of energy, such as movement, heat, sound and light.

Pole One of the two points on the Earth's surface that are farthest away from the equator. One of the two opposite ends of a **magnet**.

Protein A substance found in foods such as meat, cheese, eggs and beans. Humans and animals need protein in their diet.

Proton One of the microscopic parts of an **atom** that carries a positive **electrical charge**.

Ptyalin An **enzyme** contained in your **saliva** that breaks down the **starch** contained in food.

Pupils The round, black parts of your eyes that allow light to travel through them.

Rainbow An arch of different colors caused by sunlight shining through raindrops.

Reflection The way a wave, such as a light wave, sound wave or water wave, bounces off something else.

Retina A layer of cells on the inside of the eyeballs that is sensitive to light. The cells receive the light coming into the eye, turn it into tiny electrical signals and pass them to the brain along the **optic nerve**.

Rocket A device, usually tube shaped, containing fuels that are burned to produce hot **gases** that escape out of a rear vent, driving the device forward.

Saliva A liquid produced in your mouth that starts to break down food as you chew it. (See also **Ptyalin**.)

Salt A substance that is neither an **acid** nor a **base**. A salt is produced when an acid reacts with a base.

Satellite An object that moves around another object. Satellites around planets are prevented from floating off into space by the pull of the planet's **gravity**, but are not pulled with enough **force** to make them fall toward the planet.

Seeds The parts of a plant that can grow into new plants.

Shadow A dark shape made by something blocking out light.

Solar To do with the Sun.

Solid Something that keeps its shape rather than spreading out like a **liquid** or **gas**.

Starch A substance found in such foods as potatoes, bread and rice.

Static electricity The **electrical charge** that builds up in an object when its **atoms** lose **electrons** to other objects.

Stomata Tiny holes in the surface of a leaf through which water and **gases** pass in and out.

Surface tension A **force** that pulls together **molecules** on the surface of a **liquid**.

Taste buds A collection of tiny cells embedded in the tongue which enable us to sense the flavors of food.

Thermometer An instrument used to measure temperature.

Umbra The dark part of a **shadow** where no light reaches. (See also **Penumbra**.)

Vapor A gas, usually one that has been changed from a liquid or solid.

Veins The **blood vessels** that carry blood back to your heart from other parts of your body. (See also **Arteries**.)

Vibration The regular, to-and-fro movement of an object when it is disturbed. Guitars make sounds as a result of the vibration of their strings.

Xylem A tough tissue in a plant that draws water from the roots to the leaves. It gives support to the softer parts of the plant.

Yeast A yellowish fungus used to make bread and alcohol.

Index

Material in this book was originally developed by
Peter Adamczyk, Heather Amery, Jane Bingham, Moira Butterfield, Philip Chapman, Annabel Craig, Helen Davies, Helen Edom, Jane Elliott, Mike Flood, Anita Ganeri, Ray Gibson, Clive Gifford, Rebecca Heddle, Mark Hewish, Amanda Kent, Paul-Francis Law, Lisa Miles, Chris Oxlade, Max Parsonage, Struan Reid, Cliff Rosney, Phil Roxbee Cox, Ingrid Selberg, Paul Shipton, Richard Spurgeon, Corinne Stockley, Ruth Thomson, Rebecca Treays, Jenny Tyler, Mike Unwin, Carol Varley, Alan Ward, Gaby Waters, Fiona Watt, Lisa Watts, Jane Wertheim, Angela Wilkes, Philippa Wingate, Kate Woodward

Scientific information verified by
Max Parsonage (BSc, PGCE)

Illustrated by
Simone Abel, Andy Burton, Kuo Kang Chen, Kate Davies, Peter Dennis, Malcom English, Denise Finney, Peter Geissler, Tony Gibson, Colin King, Chris Lyon, Joseph McEwan, David Mostyn, Allan Robinson, Graham Round, John Shackell, Guy Smith, Sue Stitt

Thanks to
Mary Cartwright, Non Figg, Corinne Stockley and Carol Varley

Science equipment supplied by
Philip Harris Education, Lichfield, Staffordshire, England